JOHN HENRY HAYNES

JOHN HENRY HAYNES

A Photographer and Archaeologist in the Ottoman Empire 1881–1900

Robert G. Ousterhout

CORNUCOPIA BOOKS

FRONT COVER
Remnants of the Hittite lion gate at Aslantaş,
near Darende in southeast Anatolia, photographed
by John Henry Haynes in 1884 (plate 78)

BACK COVER
The camp at the Hittite shrine of Eflatunpınar, near
Lake Beyşehir in central Anatolia, photographed by
Haynes in 1884 or 1887 (plate 33)

INSIDE FRONT COVER
Haynes's 1892 passport. Rather than bearing
a photograph, it describes his facial features.
The first American passport was designed
by Benjamin Franklin, although only much later
did it become customary for Americans to carry one.
Haynes did not have one on his first trip abroad

INSIDE BACK COVER
A 'Special Passport' issued in 1889 after Haynes's
appointment as the first United States consul
'at Baghdad Turkey'. He received no salary
as consul, but as part of the American strategy
in Mesopotamia, he was simultaneously
hired by the University of Pennsylvania as
field manager of the excavations at Nippur

FRONTISPIECE
The Sultan Han, central Anatolia. Haynes visited
the thirteenth-century Seljuk caravanserai, on the road
from Aksaray to Konya, in 1884 and 1887 and was
the first to photograph it (plate 47)

CONTENTS

INTRODUCTION

Every picture tells a story. Sometimes it tells more than one. Take the photograph that appears as the frontispiece of this book, depicting the thirteenth-century Sultan Han, a Seljuk landmark on the road to Konya. A ruined caravanserai rises, deserted, on a barren plain. We see it from a high vantage point and a dramatic angle. Its spacious courtyard opens before us; the walls extend diagonally to meet the line of the horizon. Skeletal arcades recede into space, the vaulting long since fallen. Confronted with such desolation, the camera nevertheless captures myriad details that testify to the building's former grandeur: elegant arches and a *muqarnas* (honeycomb) vault frame the portal, now blocked; intricate geometric reliefs line the pilasters. A lone figure, almost unnoticed, stands on the roof, dwarfed by the immensity of the ruin and the vastness of the surrounding plain. The photograph is at once evocative and documentary, blending antiquarian description and visual poetics. Its melancholy mood catches our imagination – even the grainy sepia tones evoke the heat and dust of the Konya plain. We pause to contemplate the passage of time, as the carefully organised composition reveals the complexity of its subject, providing a sort of archaeological inventory of the standing remains.

There is a story behind the camera as well as in front of it. For this 1884 view of the Sultan Han – also on page 63 – the photographer John Henry Haynes (1849–1910) drew on two traditions, one old, one new: the long-standing art of landscape painting and the recent science of archaeological photography. His short apprenticeship in photography came at the hands of William James Stillman (1828–1901), as the latter recorded the Acropolis of Athens in 1881. Stillman had been trained as a painter of picturesque landscapes on the upper Hudson River of New York state and became a protégé of John Ruskin; much of Haynes's work draws on the landscape tradition. But Haynes spent a great part of his career as an excavator, and he had been instructed to become an archaeological photographer. He plied his trade on the first American Classical excavation, at Assos (1881–83) in northwest Asia Minor, and on the first American Mesopotamian excavation, at Nippur (1889–1900) in southern Iraq.

Haynes has never been included in studies of the history of photography, and although he is occasionally cited for his archaeological contributions – or dismissed for his alleged incompetence – his photography is never mentioned, while most of his few published photographs are either unattributed or credited to others. Yet his contribution remains substantial. In spite of his obscurity today, Haynes may be considered the father of American archaeological photography, the first to use the camera systematically to document ancient remains – indeed, he stands as one of the founding fathers of archaeological photography as a discipline. At Assos he was perhaps the first photographer to be included as a regular member of an excavation team. Others had certainly photographed antiquities before Haynes; some of our oldest photographs are travel views of exotic locations, such as those by Maxime du Camp or Francis Frith in Egypt and the Holy Land, but their spirit and their purposes were different.

As early as 1843, William Henry Fox Talbot, who had perfected

1A *John Henry Haynes in his 1876 yearbook photograph, when he was a student at Williams College, Massachusetts*

1B *Haynes's photography instructor, William J. Stillman, 'the American Pre-Raphaelite', drawn by Dante Gabriel Rossetti, c.1870*

1C *Haynes's nemesis, Hermann Vollrath Hilprecht, the brilliant but egotistical German-born professor of Assyriology at the University of Pennsylvania, in a studio portrait, c.1889. A victim of his own self-aggrandisement, 'the Columbus of archaeology' spent very little time in the field, but took credit and gained fame for other people's achievements*

the negative-positive procedure, recommended the documentary use of photography to record artefacts in situ before their removal. At the old Assyrian capital of Khorsabad in 1853, Gabriel Tranchard recorded the progressive uncovering of the Palace of Sargon II in a series of daguerreotypes. But these are rare examples; more often photography was used selectively. Traditionally, archaeological documentation required drawing, with the hand of the archaeological renderer as the mediator and interpreter of the site or artefact. Photography offered an entirely new, more scientific approach to documentation, from the dispassionate perspective of the camera lens. Still, there were limitations. Daguerreotypes were one of a kind, and they required an engraver or renderer to prepare mechanically reproducible images from them. Until the positive-

negative procedure became standard and publication technology developed accordingly, photography was simply the first step in the process of documentation.

At Assos, the first American excavation (1881–83), the recognition of the potential contribution of the camera was limited, and the first season passed without one. The archaeologists at Assos, notably Francis Henry Bacon (1856–1940), had been trained in the Beaux-Arts tradition of architectural rendering, and their drawings are technically accomplished, often magnificent works of art. More than sixty of Haynes's photographs appear in the Assos final report, but these were never properly credited – although he is thanked in the small print, which notes that he 'took a number of photographs of the antiquities discovered and picturesque features of the city and its vicinity'.

All the same, Bacon and others depended on his photographs for the drawings that appeared in both the preliminary and later reports – often they were no more than pen-and-ink versions of the photographs. As they saw them, the photographs were a means to an end, not the end itself.

While the work at Assos was primarily documentation, Haynes clearly knew how to take a great photograph. With little formal training – less than two months with Stillman – and no background in the visual arts, his compositional abilities still impress us. He seems to understand instinctively the theory of the picturesque that lay behind much of nineteenth-century landscape painting and photography. Perhaps because Haynes lived with the landscapes and sites he photographed, he could successfully capture their nuances and moods. Unlike the tourist or the travel photographer, determined to possess, to conquer or to dazzle, Haynes does not have a colonialist agenda; nor does he attempt to overwhelm us with spectacle and artistry. Instead, his photographs provide a unique, personal vision of a history that fascinated him in a land that he knew and loved.

EARLY LIFE

Haynes's travel and photography were made possible by the foundation of the Archaeological Institute of America (AIA) and the organisation's belief in the civilising mission of archaeology. Rather than coming from the elite circles of the educated Boston and New York gentlemen who had founded the AIA in 1879, Haynes appeared on the scene as one of the institute's first beneficiaries. He came from humble beginnings, born on January 27, 1849, on a farm in Rowe, Massachusetts, the eldest son of John W. Haynes and Emily Taylor. His family knew him as Henry, probably to distinguish him from his father, who passed away while Henry was still young. As a consequence of his father's early death, Henry delayed his education to maintain the family farm and care for his younger siblings.

In 1870, at the age of twenty-one, he enrolled at Drury Academy in North Adams to prepare himself for college. Through his own determination, he completed what was meant to be a four-year course of study in two years, then entered Williams College in nearby Williamstown in 1872. He worked his way though college as custodian of the gymnasium, where he also boarded, cooking his own meals in a small, shared room. Among his other duties, he was responsible for hauling the coal to heat the building during the cold winter months.

Several years older than his cohort and unfailingly dependable, he was nicknamed 'Daddy' by his classmates. He graduated with his class in 1876. In his graduation photograph he displays the high forehead and the prominent moustache that he sported throughout his adult life *(plate 1A)*. Trained to be a teacher, he subsequently found employment as a high school principal, first at Williamstown High School (1876–80), then briefly at South Hadley High School.

During his time at Williamstown, Haynes accompanied the Williams College professor Arthur Latham Perry as he 'critically examined' the remains of Fort Pelham, a colonial fortress near Rowe, in 1878. Although a noted economist, Perry also wrote extensively on local Massachusetts history and was an avid explorer. Perry may have been one of Haynes's instructors at Williams; at the very least Haynes was good friends with Perry's son Bliss. The examination of Fort Pelham marks Haynes's first foray into archaeology and may have sparked his interest in pursuing it further.

Haynes's life changed dramatically, however, after a chance encounter in 1880 with Charles Eliot Norton (1827–1908), a distinguished Harvard professor and the first president of the AIA. We suspect the introduction came from Perry. Recognising Haynes's interest in the ancient world, Norton offered him a position on a proposed archaeological mission to Crete. Haynes accepted immediately. One of the few significant caprices of his life, this action determined the remainder of his career. He resigned in short order from his position at South Hadley after only a few weeks of duty. He sailed from New York on February 12, 1881, travelling part of the way with Norton's teenage son Eliot, who was on his way to Turkey to assist at the other AIA-sponsored archaeological venture, at Assos, in the Troad peninsula.

As a birthday gift shortly before his departure, Haynes received a diary from his esteemed young friend Bliss Perry (1860–1954), later professor at Williams College and editor of *The Atlantic Monthly*. He kept it faithfully through his early travels. He notes in his first entry,

1D *The Haynes homestead in Rowe, with John Henry Haynes standing and his aged mother seated. The photograph must date from one of Henry's visits home in the 1880s or 90s. Only the foundations of the house survive today, while the farmland has returned to forest*

on January 28, 1881, the day after his thirty-second birthday: 'I solemnly and secretly vow with myself, John Henry Haynes, in honour of this friend that I will make it a part of daily duty to write a brief record of my feelings, success, and failures, and to read [it] occasionally, hoping to profit by this means. May I live a better life for having kept this record.' He continued the practice of daily record-keeping throughout much of his subsequent overseas travel.

Journeying by way of London and Venice, Haynes arrived in Piraeus by early March, and, after a day of sightseeing in Athens, sailed for Crete, where he met the leader of the proposed mission, William Stillman *(plate 1B)*. The AIA had the site of Knossos in mind, where a brief excavation two years earlier had exposed the storage magazines and part of the west palace façade – substantial remains of a virtually unknown ancient civilisation associated with the legendary King Minos. Stillman, in typically dramatic form, claimed to have discovered the entrance to the famed Labyrinth. Moreover, the Sublime Porte appeared to look favourably on granting the Americans a concession to excavate in Crete, which was then still part of the Ottoman Empire. In his days on the island, Haynes assisted Stillman as he photographed the landscape around Chania while they waited for the permit. After a week on the island, however, the two abruptly returned to Athens.

While the AIA had placed great hope in Stillman because of his artistic background and his familiarity with Crete, it appears he was a bit too familiar. Earlier in his career Stillman had served as the American consul in Crete, and in that capacity he had supported the failed Greek insurrection on the island of 1866–69. For overstepping his bounds as consul, he was summarily dismissed in 1868. The Ottoman authorities did not welcome his return, and it became clear that they would never support a project in which he was involved. As William C. Lawton (who excavated at Assos in 1881) later explained, the Turks believed that 'wherever Stillman did the subsoiling something younger and more explosive than archaic pottery was sure to appear'. Thus the Americans were not issued a *firman* (charter) to dig. Knossos, as is well known, was subsequently excavated by Arthur Evans in 1900 to great acclaim, earning him a knighthood, but only after Crete had effectively detached itself from the Ottoman Empire. We are left to wonder what direction American archaeology might have taken had Stillman and Haynes been successful in Crete.

Haynes accompanied Stillman back to Athens, and while waiting for further instructions from his sponsors at the AIA, he worked as Stillman's assistant. In Athens, Stillman set about photographing the monuments of the Acropolis, intending to replicate the images that had appeared in his successful folio published a decade earlier *(plates 2–5)*. In the process, Haynes learnt the technical aspects of photography from Stillman, including how to prepare and develop dry collodion plates and how to make albumen prints. The two also travelled together to Nauplion, Mycenae and Corinth, as Stillman photographed. Haynes seems to have relished this period: each diary entry begins with 'Beautiful day!' or a similar happy sentiment. At the same time, he worried about becoming a burden to the AIA, which continued to support him. In April he wrote to Charles Eliot Norton apologising for his lack of contribution to the mission of the institute, while noting that he had been 'acquiring a good knowledge and some experience under a good master'. These skills would soon prove very useful.

2 *A distant view of the Acropolis, by William J. Stillman, from his 1870 album*
'The Acropolis of Athens: Illustrated Picturesquely and Architecturally in
Photography'. Stillman isolated the sanctuary in the distance, with a windmill
in the foreground and the Temple of Olympian Zeus in the middle ground

3 *Also from Stillman's 1870 album is this striking composition – half*
a view into space, half solid marble temple – showing the curvature of the
Parthenon's stylobate, the steps on which the columns stand. Haynes learnt
the rudiments of picturesque photography from accompanying Stillman

4 *Another plate from Stillman's 1870 Athens album. From the entablature, above the columns, he captures a dramatic perspective of the Parthenon frieze leading to a glimpse of the city below in the distance*

5 *A very similar view of the Parthenon frieze taken in 1881, either by Stillman or Haynes, unattributed but part of Haynes's personal collection. The angle of view has shifted very slightly from the earlier photograph so that more of the frieze is exposed*

SAILING TO ASSOS

A FOOTHOLD IN THE EAST

While Haynes was working on the Acropolis in Athens with Stillman in late March 1881, young Eliot Norton had happened by, and he subsequently escorted Haynes and Stillman to Piraeus to meet his travelling companion, Joseph Thacher Clarke (1856–1920). The two were on their way to Assos (Behramkale), where Clarke was to direct the excavation and Norton was to be his assistant. Haynes offered his services to the Assos expedition but was initially rebuffed by Clarke, as the permit to excavate had not yet been issued. Clarke and Norton sailed on, and Haynes remained in Athens with Stillman for the time being. Norton Senior apparently reconsidered Haynes's assignment. On May 18, Haynes left Athens for Smyrna (Izmir), on his way to Assos by way of Mytilene.

The deciding factor seems to have been Haynes's newly acquired knowledge of photography. Following the arrival of Haynes, a camera and the necessary chemicals were ordered from England in June, but they were not to arrive until November, after the first season had ended. As William C. Lawton would explain in his account of the expedition, 'This comrade had learned the art of photography from his former chief, and if any apparatus had arrived for him, he would have been the photographer of the expedition.'

Assos remains one of the most attractive ancient Greek sites, set dramatically on the rocky outcropping on the shore of the Troad peninsula overlooking the island of Lesbos. Haynes later wrote in his journal that when the acropolis became visible from a distance, the sight 'was enough to thrill anyone who had learned to love its beauties'. Like his expedition co-director, Francis Henry Bacon, Clarke had studied architecture, and both were fascinated by the Classical orders, particularly the development of the Doric order. Two years previously, in 1879, they had travelled around the Aegean on a sailing boat – aptly named the *Dorian* – examining all known Doric temple sites.

When the two stopped at Assos, they were impressed by the substantial remains of the archaic Temple of Athena on the acropolis, which seemed to hold a key position in the early formation of the Doric order. Impressive remains of the city walls, theatre, agora, public buildings and cemetery were also visible. With support from the AIA, a team of eight young men, most of them fresh from Harvard, had assembled in April 1881. Haynes joined them, full of enthusiasm, but the start of the first season had stalled, for the *irade* (authorisation) to excavate was not issued by the Ministry of Public Instruction until midsummer.

In addition to surveying the site, the young men explored the coastal areas and climbed Mount Ida. Once excavation began, they took turns overseeing the workmen. Even without a camera, Haynes could make himself useful, and the others came to value his judgment. Several years older, and from a considerably less privileged background than his colleagues, he was nicknamed 'the Professor'.

While periodically tormented by locusts, fleas, fevers, digestive ailments, oppressive heat and local quarrels, Haynes seems to have thoroughly enjoyed the adventure and thenceforth styled himself an archaeologist. He was not even discouraged by the professional misconduct of Clarke, who disappeared for weeks on end, apparently to the sensual pleasures of Smyrna, leaving the rest of the team on site with neither financial means nor provisions. The other Americans from the first season, all volunteers, refused to return. One of the team, Charles Wesley Bradley, died three years later, at the age of twenty-seven, the result of complications from malaria contracted at Assos.

By the end of October, the excavation had wound down, and most of the Americans gradually departed. In early November, Haynes and a companion made their way to Çanakkale, on the Dardanelles, where they boarded a steamer to Constantinople (Istanbul). Almost immediately Haynes was hired as a tutor at Robert College. It appears that someone had written on his behalf, and to his surprise he was expected. Located above Rumelihisarı and established on the American university model in 1863, Robert College appeared as a bit of New England on the Bosphorus *(plate 22)*. Haynes collected his trunk and settled in. He taught English and Latin for the next three years, although his salary as tutor was minimal – 'it's considered to be a missionary enterprise,' he explained in a letter to Norton – but he expressed his intention of remaining in the Ottoman Empire until he had seen more of the fascinating historic areas around him.

Haynes's correspondence during this period is filled with ideas about explorations ranging from nearby Bithynia to distant Syria and Palestine. An expedition to Syria seemed a real possibility, and Haynes set to work to determine its cost. But with such a negligible income, he was at the mercy of potential sponsors, and his only marketable talent was his photography. Even at this he was limited, for he did not own a camera. The one in his possession belonged to the AIA, but fortunately they continued to underwrite his travels. At Robert College, he found a supportive community *(plates 23 and 24)*, as well as access to a darkroom for printing the pictures.

He returned to the excavations at Assos during the summers of 1882 and 1883 to photograph. But the heat was not favourable to photography, and his training had been limited to the two months he had spent as Stillman's assistant. In addition to his own inexperience, Haynes's efforts were plagued by poor-quality chemicals, inferior papers, the slowness of deliveries of materials, and the limited time he could spend away from the college. His letters are full of lengthy apologies for his shortcomings in the darkroom and equally lengthy explanations of the technical aspects of photography he was struggling to master. Gelatine plates seemed to work better than collodion plates, he wrote, although both could melt in his hands if prepared incorrectly or exposed under improper circumstances; however, the glass plates could be washed and the chemicals reapplied; photographs could be taken again and again if time allowed; ultimately the value of negatives depended not on their appearance but on what they could print, which could often only be determined in the darkroom. Nevertheless, several hundred photographic views are preserved from his efforts in those two summers, many of them quite stunning. Today we see the early excavations at Assos primarily through the eyes of Haynes.

6　*Haynes's first photographic assignment was the American excavation
at Assos, near Troy, on Turkey's northern Aegean coast. This view of
the harbour seen from above was taken in 1882 or 1883. The Americans
rented two rooms in one of the warehouses as their living quarters*

7 *Approaching the Ottoman harbour at Assos from the sea, with the
ancient city and its acropolis rising above, 1882 or 1883. The finds from the
first American venture into Classical archaeology are divided between
the Istanbul Archaeological Museum and the Boston Museum of Fine Arts*

8 *A view of the acropolis at Assos (Behramkale) seen from a distance in 1883, with Haynes's companion, the epigrapher John Robert Sitlington Sterrett, sitting in the roadway for no apparent reason*

9 *Excavating along the rear wall of the South Stoa, which formed a retaining wall for the terrace of the agora (marketplace). Much of the work at Assos aimed to clean and document the standing remains. Haynes's 1882 photograph shows the Classical wall at a dramatic angle, with the local labourers posing and the German archaeologist Robert Koldewey seated in the shadows on the left*

22 JOHN HENRY HAYNES

10 *The archaeologist Joseph Thacher Clarke examining the corbelled arch of Gate 10, in the eastern wall of Assos, 1882 or 1883. The Archaeological Institute of America had high hopes for Clarke, but he ultimately disappointed them with his unprofessional behaviour, leaving the final report to others to complete*

11 *A village boy leans against a wall that reveals three different periods of masonry (from the sixth to the fourth century BC). Haynes took this photograph of 1882 or 1883 near Gate 2, in the western wall*

12 *A young boy peeks from behind a wall between tomb monuments in the west necropolis at Assos, 1882 or 1883. Haynes often introduces locals almost as an alternative subject to the archaeological remains*

13 *A lone horseman is dramatically silhouetted against the sky on the early Ottoman bridge east of ancient Assos, 1882 or 1883*

14 *A worker poses in the shade of an umbrella next to a brilliantly lit rock-cut tomb at Assos, 1882 or 1883. The shot offers interesting contrasts in shapes, with the man's head mimicking the round shape at the head of the anthropomorphic tomb*

15 *A barefoot worker on the Assos acropolis rests on top of an archaic Doric capital from the Temple of Athena, 1882 or 1883*

16 *A local archaeologist, distinctly non-Classical in appearance, poses uncomfortably on top of a Late Antique inscribed statue base at Assos, 1882 or 1883*

17 *Workers with pieces of the temple frieze found in the village at Assos, 1882 or 1883. Fascinated by the early Doric temple on the acropolis, the archaeologists recovered enough pieces of the fallen structure to reconstruct its original form. Unusually for the Doric order, the temple included a frieze on its architrave. The pieces shown here, depicting hunters in pursuit of centaurs, were found in 1881; those to the left are now in the Istanbul Archaeological Museum, and the piece on the right is in the Boston Museum of Fine Arts*

18 *The archaeologist Francis Henry Bacon poses in the excavated Roman*
tomb monument of Publius Varius, in the west necropolis, 1882 or 1883.
Bacon ultimately brought the Assos excavation report to fruition, married
Alice Mary Calvert, the daughter of Frank Calvert, who had discovered Troy,
and spent much of the rest of his life in the area

19 *The archaeologist Robert Koldewey strikes a contemplative pose before the walls of Assos, 1882 or 1883*

20 *Assos, 1882 or 1883. Haynes employs a marble pilaster capital*
as a pedestal for three fragmentary sculpted heads of different periods,
posed to suggest a conversation in progress

21 *Haynes poses three Hellenistic clay figurines from Assos on a book,*
like dolls at a tea party, 1882 or 1883

CONSTANTINOPLE

22 Founded in 1863 by American philanthropists, Robert College appears
as a bit of New England dramatically perched on a hill above the Bosphorus.
It offered students, without distinction of race or religion, an education based
on the principles of a 'first-class American college'. Haynes was a tutor in
English and Latin there from 1881 to 1884

23 Haynes poses with his fellow teachers from Robert College on a picnic
somewhere on the Bosphorus. He stands third from the right in the back row,
his high forehead and prominent moustache easily identifiable

24 *Yoros Castle, Istanbul, 1881–84. Colleagues from Robert College pose before the blocked gateway of this Byzantine fortress above the Bosphorus. Located on the Asian shore, overlooking the Black Sea, Yoros (Anadolu Kavağı) remains a popular destination for weekend excursions*

TRAVELS WITH A CAMERA
ANATOLIA, SYRIA AND MESOPOTAMIA

The trip to Syria did not come to fruition as Haynes had planned. Instead, the epigrapher and historical geographer John Robert Sitlington Sterrett (1851–1914) proposed an excursion to Cappadocia during the summer of 1884, which the AIA had agreed to underwrite. Sterrett was interested in collecting inscriptions and milestones and in adding to the cartography of the region, which the German Heinrich Kiepert had begun. Haynes and Sterrett knew each other from the excavations at Assos, where Sterrett had studied the inscriptions in the 1883 season. Following their Anatolian journey, the two travelled to Mesopotamia together on the Wolfe Expedition, and they were to stay in regular contact for years afterwards. Sterrett held a PhD from Munich, and immediately before their rendezvous in June 1884, he had been exploring the hinterland of Smyrna with the noted historical geographer Sir William Ramsay – which is to say, Sterrett was a recognised scholar with better connections and better academic credentials than Haynes.

Travel in the Ottoman hinterland in the 1880s was at best difficult, often painfully slow, and occasionally dangerous. Rail travel was limited. Roads were of inferior quality and not maintained. In the interior, most were not suitable for carriages. In many areas they were not well marked, and it was easy to lose one's way; Haynes's diaries record assorted mistakes, backtracking and nights spent unintentionally in the open. Unused to adventurers, the local inhabitants were often suspicious. Bandits made some areas unsafe to explore without a paid *zaptiye*, or gendarme. Servants, guards and pack animals had to be hired and fed *(plate 29)*. While some fresh foodstuffs could be found along the way, there was no guarantee of their availability, so basic provisions had to be carried as well. Lodgings were difficult to find and rarely clean; *hans* (caravanserais) and village guest rooms were spartan at best and often infested with fleas and lice *(plates 30–31)*. More often than not, Haynes and Sterrett opted to sleep on the roof. Journeying with crates of fragile photographic plates only added to the complexity. Not surprisingly, Haynes was the first to photograph many of the inland archaeological sites.

From their rendezvous in Akşehir, Haynes and Sterrett travelled to the Hittite shrine at Eflatunpınar and the Seljuk capital at Konya, and Haynes took numerous photographs at both sites. These are the earliest photos of Eflatunpınar *(plates 33–34)*, and they had been specifically requested by the AIA; they may also be the earliest taken at Konya *(plates 36–43)*. The two then travelled by way of the Sultan Han *(plates 44–47)*, then across Cappadocia *(plates 48–67)* to Kayseri *(plates 68–70)*, where they visited the American missionaries at Talas. There Haynes deposited a supply of glass plate negatives to be collected on their return trip. The two then continued eastwards, as Sterrett hunted for Roman milestones and ancient inscriptions. They ventured as far east as Malatya, before returning by way of Kayseri across Cappadocia, and then turned northwards to the Hittite site of Boğazköy *(plate 71)*, then to Ankara *(plates 72–75)*, where their journey effectively terminated. In his *Preliminary Report on an Epigraphical Journey Made in Asia Minor*, published the following year, Sterrett noted that Haynes had taken 320 photographs during their travels together.

Haynes's photographs are accompanied by letters and diary entries recording his impressions of people and landscapes, as well as the mundane details of travel. When I say mundane, I mean mundane. A typical entry:

Monday July 21st [1884]

After a night of restlessness I rose 3:30 and began some mending I had to do & about 4:30 ate my breakfast & started out to photograph an ancient gate or door called by the natives Allah Kapou and fragment of a wall now built into Gregorian Armenian church but once belonged to a Christian church of Roman times as far as present appearances now indicate.

Sterrett rose later than I and copied a worthless inscription in a mill just below the village. A few minutes before 7 a.m. we direct our course down the Sarus past the Circassian village where we staid [sic] last Friday night. Did not pass near to it but at some distance. Saw a great number of Circassians cutting hay with their rude scythes. Though hard at work in the broiling sun they did not remove any of their warm clothing but had their coats full buttoned and their black wool and fur caps without any kind of protection for the eyes.

Travelling on and on with nothing to eat and no villages after 9 o'clock we arrived in Hadjin about 4 o'clock.

Not the most compelling of diarists, Haynes reveals little in his writing of the sensitivity evident in his photographs: he will belabour the less-than-satisfactory conditions of lodgings, the

25 *Perhaps the first photograph of the Palmyra Gate, principal entrance to the Syrian caravan city of Dura-Europos on the Euphrates, 1885. Abandoned after the Sassanian siege of AD 256–57, Dura was officially 'discovered' in 1898*

quality of the breakfast, the weather, and especially the best way to pack glass negatives. The last was a real concern, however, for damage to the plates meant the failure of his enterprise. Thus:

If the glass plates are put up according to the English method in millboard boxes of one dozen each they should be packed in the following way and no harm will come to them on pack animals. Put 4 doz. plates neatly put up in cardboard boxes into a wooden box fitted to them to allow a very little straw about their edges not on the flat sides. Four of these boxes should then be put into another strong box, well bound, and the cover fastened with screws.

In fact, it was good that he took such care, as he records the following incident on the 1884 journey:

Our Albanian and the cook had charge of the baggage. The Albanian came in with two horses saying that the cook was behind with an injured horse and two others… The account given was that the horse, which was perhaps the steadiest, stumbled, his pack shifted, his saddle turned, he became frightened and began kicking. His load happened to be the two boxes containing plates. They were thrown one rolling one way and the other going the other way and certainly the boxes showed hard usage. All the joints of one box had started very considerably and even the little boxes within were not free from damage in the same respect. However I could not see that any injury had happened to the plates. But for this we must wait and see.

In spite of the concern for detail evident in entries like this one, Haynes often forgot to note place names and is maddeningly brief concerning the sites he visited, presumably relying on his photographs to fill in the details. Only occasionally do the mundane daily activities figure in his photography, as for example when his companion Sterrett got a shave in a *han (plate 28)*.

Haynes usually kept a log of his photographs. His records for 1885, for example, note not just the location or subject but the type of plate used, time of day, weather conditions and length of exposure. A typical entry, for the gate at Dura-Europos *(plate 25)*, reads as follows: '164 (W&W) 22. Instantaneous. 7 or 8 sec, thick cloudy, half an hour after sun rise April 3rd. Walls and towers of Sassanian city 9 hours below Meadheen at Salahiya. Overexposure.'

The entry requires a bit of unpacking to make sense. Haynes

numbered the photographs individually per journey, then 1 to 24, as the glass negatives were apparently packed two dozen at a time. He listed the platemaker (here W&W stands for Wratten and Wainwright, London) and type (here Instantaneous – as opposed to Ordinary – gelatin dry plates, for rapid exposure). Finally, he gives the site name, al-Mayadin at as-Salhiyah (Deir ez-Zur).

While he fussed over exposure times and the qualities of the plates, Haynes was developing a critical eye for landscapes. He was particularly captivated by Cappadocia, visiting the region again in 1887. He took dozens of photographs in the areas around Selime in 1884 (plates 48, 52–53), where Haynes and Sterrett seem to have been the first Westerners to record a visit to the site. They also visited Göreme and the Soğanlı Valley, following in the footsteps of William Hamilton, who recorded his travels through the region in the 1830s. Haynes seems to have been more interested in the curious landforms than the architecture. Nevertheless, his photos are valuable documents. For example, the rock-cut Tomb 10 at Avcılar (Göreme) has since been disfigured by erosion (plate 54), and the façade of the Bezirhane complex at the same site has subsequently collapsed (plate 55). Both are now enveloped by a prosperous tourist town. At Çavuşin, he recorded the rock-cut village before its collapse and abandonment (plate 56), and his photographs of Ürgüp record the construction of modern buildings at the base of the plateau – now a historic district (plate 63).

In his journal, Haynes recorded his first impressions of the region, where he bedded down on the roof of his lodgings at Selime and seems to have been too excited to sleep:

… here with the bright moon light to make night seem like day one feels rather like studying and admiring these wonderful abodes of past generations than like closing his wondering eyes in dreamy slumber, and yet it seems well nigh impossible to quiet one's excited feelings with such surroundings. Altogether these rock formations and the multitude of excavated dwellings … appear to me now the most wonderful thing I have ever been permitted to rest my eyes upon in all my travels and among all the wonderfully interesting things it has been my good fortune to see in the land of wonders.' (Journal 3, 1884)

He continues in this vein for several more pages, as he accepts the opinion that these were the dwellings of Christians fleeing persecution. Although he contemplated writing a book about the volcanic region, this was never realised. In a letter to his family in October 1885 he writes:

I am unfortunate enough to have more reputation as a photographer than I want: for my friends call upon me pretty frequently and I have in this way done a good deal but I do not like it. It makes a drudge of me and unfits me for any literary work. I ought moreover to find time for study and to work up into a treatise last summer's investigations among the cave dwellers of Asia Minor. But as yet have not found the requisite time to do so. Pres. Norton urges me to write up some of my experiences for the American Journal of Archaeology and I ought to do it or give up archaeological work forever.

While his book never came to fruition, many of his photographs from the 1884 trip ended up as the property of his travelling companion, Sterrett, who appears in several of them. Sterrett gives a good sense of what Haynes's unwritten treatise might have been like in several essays, including 'Troglodyte Dwellings in Cappadocia', published in *The Century Magazine* in 1900, and a 1919 article in *The National Geographic Magazine* entitled 'The Cone Dwellers of Asia Minor: A Primitive People Who Live in Nature-Made Apartment Houses Fashioned by Volcanic Violence and Trickling Streams'. In these he compares the inhabitants of Cappadocia to primitive, uncivilised cavemen, drawing comparisons from ancient texts, such as Diodorus Siculus's fanciful account of the races of the extreme south, the Ethiopians and the Troglodytes, which he quotes at length: they drink blood, run around naked, kill the aged and infirm and make merry at funerals. Herodotus, Xenophon and the Old Testament are quoted to similar effect. Moreover, Sterrett mocks the credulity of earlier European travellers to the region, and in the end he supposes it is a Bronze Age settlement with a few Byzantine intrusions.

The 1900 article included ten drawings 'after photographs by the author' that look suspiciously like Haynes's pictures. The 1919 article was illustrated with no fewer than 52 of Haynes's photographs, from this journey as well as from a second journey

Haynes took alone in 1887 – but alas, all are credited to Sterrett. The latter article appeared several years after the deaths of both men, so Sterrett may not be completely at fault, but it seems to have been Haynes's fate that his work would be credited to others. We can be certain that these are his photographs, because they match those he kept in his possession and those that appeared in his 1892 folio. Moreover, Haynes's journal regularly records Sterrett going ahead to find inscriptions while he stayed behind to photograph the monuments and landscapes. Viewed more positively, Haynes's photographs could make a splash more than thirty years after he took them – and, indeed, long after he was dead.

After his excursion with Sterrett, Haynes returned briefly to Constantinople before setting out again, this time on the Wolfe Expedition, for which he had been hired as business manager and photographer. Mrs Catherine Lorillard Wolfe of New York had given $5,000 to defray the cost of an exploratory expedition to Babylonia under the leadership of the indefatigable Rev. Dr William Hayes Ward (1835–1916), clergyman, Orientalist and subsequent editor of the New York *Independent*. Sterrett and an Armenian translator, Daniel Z. Noorian, completed the team. Joseph Thacher Clarke was supposed to go as well, but ever the delinquent, he backed out at the last minute.

They sailed from Constantinople to Mersin at the end of October 1884, then travelled overland to visit ancient sites in southeast Anatolia before heading eastward into Mesopotamia *(plates 76–85)*, often enjoying the hospitality of American missions along the way. At the Mardin mission, they signed the guestbook, identifying themselves as 'the Wolfe gang'.

At Carchemish, which had been investigated by the British Museum in 1878–81, Haynes took several photographs – the earliest of the site – while his colleagues briefly examined the orthostat reliefs left behind by the British. In one view, Ward (or possibly Sterrett) appears copying the inscription identifying the seated figure of Bonus-tis, Queen of Carchemish, with the winged Naked Goddess to the right *(plate 83)*. The panel was still complete in 1880, when the British Consul Patrick Henderson attempted to have it removed but succeeded only in breaking it into three pieces. In another photograph, their translator Daniel Z. Noorian appears sitting awkwardly amid fragments of the processional frieze, between a genie and the broken paws of a lion *(plate 82)*. Ward related that the upper portion of the genie had fallen, and it took four men to lift it into place before it could be photographed. Typical of Haynes, who liked to introduce a sort of mirroring into his images, the lion's paws are mimicked by Noorian's gloved hands, folded on his knees. Sadly, when Haynes returned to Carchemish four years later, he found the upper portion of the genie broken into pieces, and by the time the British resumed excavations in 1911, the fragments had disappeared. In the later reports, the excavators relied on Haynes's photograph, although the published image was cropped, showing only the left third, eliminating the sitter, but not his extended right foot, as well as the lion's paws.

In December they visited Mosul and Erbil and were particularly impressed by the remains at the latter. However, Sterrett fell gravely ill at Erbil, and they pushed on to Baghdad, where he was placed under the care of the British consul, and the others were forced to continue without him. Throughout the region, they were impressed by the great mounds, remnants of ancient cities, palaces and temples *(plate 84)*. South of Babylon they entered areas no American had previously traversed, and no European for several decades.

The purpose of the explorations was to find a suitable site for an American excavation in Babylonia. Many Americans had become fascinated with the ancient cultures of the region, whose rich body of literature was known from the cuneiform scripts only recently translated. Many episodes in Mesopotamian mythology seemed to parallel Old Testament events: for example, both preserved a tradition of a great flood. Scientific exploration of the region, it was thought, might support the veracity of the Bible.

In southern Mesopotamia, they visited the site of Nuffar, ancient Nippur, a sacred Sumerian site, which seemed to have potential for discovery. As they headed north again, Sterrett was recovered enough to join them for the return journey. They made the month-long desert crossing by way of Dura-Europos and Palmyra. At the former, which Haynes identified simply as 'Sassanian city', he photographed the impressive city gate *(plate 25)* – the site was not officially 'discovered' for another thirteen years – and at the latter he photographed at the request of the AIA. According to Haynes, the Orientalist Ward 'cared nothing for Palmyra before coming', but 'was delighted with the ample ruins here'. Accordingly they

26 *Sterrett, apparently recovered from the serious illness that had stranded him in Baghdad, strikes a pose amid the ruins of Palmyra, 1885*

extended their stay, allowing Haynes to take almost a hundred photographs. They continued to Damascus and finally Beirut, where they effectively ended their explorations in April 1885. Ward returned to New York, taking with him their young translator Noorian – who lived with Ward's family and subsequently became a prominent art and antiquities dealer in New York City. Sterrett headed to Athens, and Haynes to Constantinople.

Ward quickly published an enthusiastic account of their expedition, but it was several years before his recommendations for further exploration and archaeology were acted upon. While Ottoman laws governing foreign excavations had recently become more restrictive, Ward felt that either Anbar in the north or Nuffar in the south held great potential for exploration; even without a permit to excavate, mapping and surface documentation could be of great value. And if antiquities could not be excavated, he noted, at the very least they could be purchased in the bazaar.

The changes in antiquities laws came about under the looming presence of Osman Hamdi Bey (1842–1910), artist, diplomat and director of the Imperial Museum in Constantinople *(plate 101)*, who rewrote the law governing antiquities in 1883–84, restricting foreign excavations and prohibiting archaeological finds from leaving Ottoman territory. Rather than dividing the artefacts, as had been done in the past, this change meant that Hamdi Bey's museum became the repository of all new discoveries from within the boundaries of the Ottoman Empire. Moreover, Hamdi Bey became the gatekeeper to whom all foreign archaeologists had to answer. Rather than continue to allow the Empire to be the passive setting for foreign excavators and treasure-hunters, Hamdi Bey had shifted the balance of power, effectively laying claim to all archaeological sites within the Ottoman Empire. The Americans, arriving late on the scene and anxious to catch up with their European colleagues and to fill their own museums with antiquities, were understandably distressed by this turn of events.

Although the new antiquities law appeared rigid in its terms, it was more flexible in practice: 'gifts' could be presented to obliging foreign archaeologists as part of Hamdi Bey's diplomatic strategy. The American excavations at Assos had been undertaken before the law was rewritten, and the AIA had hoped to substantially enrich the Boston Museum of Fine Arts (MFA). But Clarke had bungled the negotiations for the division of artefacts, and his effrontery had so offended Hamdi Bey that he had not issued the export permit. Crates were still sitting on the beach at Assos two years after the completion of the excavations, and in the end the MFA received only thirteen of more than forty promised crates of antiquities. Haynes had to intervene, presenting copies of publications and photographs to placate Hamdi Bey. Haynes was hardly of the same stature as the aristocratic Hamdi Bey, and Professor Alexander van Millingen of Robert College accompanied him on his missions of conciliation.

To participate in the Wolfe Expedition, Haynes had resigned his position as tutor at Robert College. He subsequently found employment as treasurer and instructor at Central Turkey College, part of the American Board of Christian Foreign Missions, in Aintab (now Gaziantep), where he was based for the next three years *(plate 27)*. The Wolfe Expedition had spent many pleasant days with the Aintab missionaries, and Haynes found himself at home in the town. There might even have been a love interest there, as his Philadelphia associates later suspected. Always short of funds, however, Haynes now found himself responsible for the finances of an institution even more economically challenged than himself. His official correspondence from this period reflects the daily struggles to keep the impoverished and understaffed school in operation. 'The college is still hard pressed and before the present term is ended will be still more pressed,' he begins a letter of April 20, 1886, to W. W. Peet at the American Board office in Constantinople. Nevertheless, the location of Aintab placed Haynes in an ideal position for archaeological excursions into a region only beginning to be explored. In the same letter, he jokes, 'Our vacation journey went off well. Discovered subterranean galleries older than the creation of man. You can imagine our disappointment.'

Haynes set out on a second road trip in mid-July of 1887, covering more than a thousand miles in two months *(see map, plate 86)*. This time he was supported by the architect William R. Ware (1832–1915), the first professor of architecture at Massachusetts Institute of Technology and subsequently founder of the School of Architecture at Columbia University. He was also an active supporter of the AIA. Charles Eliot Norton put up the money for improved camera equipment. Haynes had planned this trip himself and, without Sterrett, he assumed the role of archaeologist in charge. From the antiquities around Aintab, the trip took him through Lycaonia and Cappadocia and into Phrygia.

Haynes's tour was specifically for the purpose of photographing archaeological sites, to produce a folio of images for commercial sale. He revisited several locations from his 1884 tour, including Eflatunpınar, Cappadocia and Kayseri. While the folio lists all photographs as coming from the 1887 travels, it actually included images gathered on both journeys.

There was growing interest at the time in the Hittites and Phrygians and other obscure early peoples of Anatolia. During this trip Haynes took measurements at many of the monuments he visited, as at Eflatunpınar, where he notes simply, 'Took photos and measured the huge pile. Found it difficult to climb to the top and get down safely.' Later he realised he had forgotten some of the measurements but determined these could be scaled from the recorded measurements and the photographs – that is, he realised the photogrammetric potential of the camera *(plates 34 and 35)*. At the rock relief at Ivriz it was necessary to construct a scaffold

27 *The Central Turkey College at Aintab (Gaziantep) was Haynes's home for the years 1885–87, when he served as teacher and treasurer for the missionary school. Founded in 1874, the college moved to Aleppo in 1924, where it continued as Aleppo College*

in order to photograph and measure the sculptures; he reports that the god stands 13ft 11in tall *(plate 88)*.

The ultimate goal of Haynes's 1887 trip was the highlands of Phrygia, to record the rock-cut monuments around the so-called City of Midas *(plates 92–95)*. Photographs of the area had been requested specifically by his patron, and Haynes, with a limited budget and limited time, often cut his journey short elsewhere to hasten towards Phrygia. Most (but certainly not all) of these monuments survive in more or less the condition in which Haynes recorded them. Not so elsewhere.

His few photographs from Binbirkilise, the so-called 'Thousand and One Churches' on the skirts of the extinct volcano of Karadağ, are perhaps his most valuable, although his record is frustratingly brief *(plates 89–91)*. The early Byzantine site in Lycaonia is best known from the photographs of Gertrude Bell, who studied the site and its many churches with Sir William Ramsay in 1907. But an earthquake seems to have levelled many of the buildings in the lower city sometime between Haynes's visit and Bell's. Thus Haynes's photographs clarify numerous aspects of these buildings

Turkish barber shaving Prof Sterrett on corridor of Khan

28 *A Turkish barber shaves Sterrett in the corridor of the 'han' in Malatya, to the apparent fascination of local men, 1884*

unknown to Bell. Haynes's photograph of Churches 8 and 13 *(plate 90)* is taken from the southeast, whereas Bell's is from the northwest. By the time Bell had arrived on the scene, no. 8 had fallen but was still recognisable, while no. 13 was nothing but a pile of rubble, so much so that she did not bother to record it. Haynes's view is our only photographic record of no. 13. Scholars have long been interested in the octagonal Church 8 because of its similarities to the martyrium described by Gregory of Nyssa. Haynes's photograph confirms that this was indeed an impressive building, and typically, Haynes posed his travelling companions in the windows.

Haynes had to cut short his visit to Binbirkilise on August 3, 1887, having photographed only four or five of its buildings. He wrote in a letter to Ware, two years later, 'Since there was no water within several miles and the sun was very hot I could only take a few photographs as speedily as possible and hasten away to join the caravan.' More critically, it seems, there was no food for the horses.

Sadly, results were not forthcoming. Haynes had envisaged a folio of images to be sold commercially, perhaps following the model of Stillman's Acropolis folio. But the pictures still needed to be printed, and both time and the necessary chemicals and papers were in short supply in Aintab. He considered hiring a local man to do the printing for him. Finally, the folio appeared in 1892, with a selection of 120 photographs, some badly printed. Judging from its general obscurity, it was not a commercial success. The small brochure published to accompany the folio included a map of his route *(plate 86)*; the photographs range from southeast Anatolia to Phrygia. Haynes's lingering fascination with Cappadocia dominates both the folio and the brochure text. He included forty-seven views of the eroded and rock-cut features of the region, writing in the brief introduction:

> *Who were the first occupants of these wonderful caves we do not know; but from the appearance of the excavations themselves we judge them to have been made in very ancient times by a race of people of whom we know very little. Whatever we may think of the origins of these peculiar habitations it is certain from the churches and chapels of the Byzantine period that they were once occupied by Christians. It is also reasonable to suppose that the persecutions of the Roman emperors drove these early Christians from the coasts of Asia Minor to this obscure region where they could live in concealment in these abandoned dwellings.*

The folio contained some impressive views but also evidence of haste and lack of vision in its organisation. It begins with a Hittite rock inscription, for which a translation is not offered, and which is not one of Haynes's most compelling images *(plate 87)*. For Cappadocia, some of the photographs are repetitious and grainy, possibly made with paper negatives *(see, for example, plate 62)* – he discussed at length the advantages and disadvantages of paper negatives in his correspondence. He also included for no apparent reason forgeries of antiquities he was offered in Kayseri. The folio concludes with views of Qalaat Saman *(plates 96–98)* and Aleppo in Syria, although neither is included on the map of his 1887 route, and it is unclear when he visited those sites. Throughout, the captions tend to be vague and unenlightening.

The 1892 folio stands as something of a swansong for Haynes's travel photography. He envisaged a folio of images, which two years after the trip he was still unable to produce. Moreover, Haynes realised that the rapid advances in scholarship were passing

29 In the 1880s Haynes travelled several times with the noted epigrapher John Robert Sitlington Sterrett. Haynes photographed while Sterrett collected inscriptions. In this photograph, taken somewhere in Anatolia in 1884, their party sets off, with Sterrett (in white with a pith helmet) bringing up the rear. In his 'Preliminary Report on an Epigraphical Journey', Sterrett notes that Haynes had taken 320 photos during their travels that summer

him by. His privileged colleagues had begun their studies at a younger age than he had, were better educated and had good libraries at their disposal. While neither Bacon nor Clarke sought careers in archaeology, Sterrett, ensconced in the newly founded American School of Classical Studies at Athens, went on to become professor of Greek at Cornell in 1901. His young friend from Williamstown, Bliss Perry, was by that time teaching at Williams and would later move to Princeton. Haynes lamented, 'Neither money nor leisure nor books are at my command. In these days of the rapid growth of scholarship… to write anything of

permanent value, one must consult the writings of others…'

In a letter of March 17, 1886, he begs W. W. Peet to sell him Hamilton's *Researches in Asia Minor* from the Bible House Library in Constantinople. 'I would give more for that book than any book I know of,' he wrote. 'It would be worth more to me than almost any book that is published.' Apparently he was unsuccessful – the book is still in the Bible House Library collection. By the end of 1888, Haynes had become drawn into the difficult, isolated and problematic excavations at Nuffar/Nippur, and these consumed – some might argue, destroyed – the remainder of his career.

30 *A 'han', or caravanserai, in Malatya, 1884, typical of the accommodation used by travellers in the late Ottoman Empire. The 'han' had rooms organised round the courtyard, with space for storage and animals on the lower level and chambers for guests on the upper level*

31 *Haynes and Sterrett often chose to sleep on the roof of the 'han', having found the rooms infested with vermin. In this 1884 photograph, the travellers are just beginning to rouse themselves at dawn*

33 *Eflatunpınar ('Plato's Spring'), a Hittite shrine from 1300 BC, on Lake Beyşehir, west of Konya. Ottoman folk belief credited Plato with building the shrine as a talisman to protect residents of the Konya area from floods. Haynes, the first person to photograph the site, was there in 1884 and 1887*

FOLLOWING PAGES
34 *Haynes took great care to photograph Eflatunpınar without the distortions of perspective, even setting up his tripod in the frigid spring water for this photograph, probably taken in 1887*
35 *A page from Haynes's notebook for 1887, with a measured drawing*

32 *A crowd gathers at a village inn for a group photograph, probably taken in central Anatolia in 1884 when Haynes was on his way to Mesopotamia*

EFLATUNPINAR

Monday Aug. 8. 1887

An awful wind made the tent an uncomfortable place to sleep stay in. Could not sleep until the wind died away a morning. Hastily took the necessary photographs sent off the baggage. Mustapher and I followed overtaking them at noon. Arrived at Teflatun Punar about 3 p.m. A stream half as large and strong as that at Ivris makes green banks frequented by a multitude of cattle, mares with their colts, sheep & goats. Took the photos. and measured the huge pile. Found it difficult to climb to the top and get down safely

Upper Stone at Teflatun 22 ft. 7 inches long. 4 ft thick.. 3 ft 8½ inches high. Second long Stone about 14 feet long

KONYA

36 *Konya's Alaeddin Camii seen from the north, 1884. The throne mosque
for the Seljuk Sultans of Rum (Anatolia) contained their dynastic mausolea,
and was built in stages in the twelfth and thirteenth centuries. On the right are
the remains of a Seljuk kiosk (now destroyed), once part of Alaeddin
Keykubad's palace; the area in between is filled with ruins of the palace*

37 *Haynes employed shadows and diagonals to dramatic effect on Monument
Hill, as he called the citadel of Konya – the mound at the centre of the Seljuk
capital. In this 1884 photograph the Alaeddin Camii is seen from the east*

38 *The north façade of the Alaeddin Camii, Konya, 1884. The portal,*
here boarded over, is surrounded by elegant Seljuk polychrome carvings and
reused Byzantine window mullions

39 *The Sahip Ata Camii (1285), Konya, 1884. The lavish detailing of the façade is characteristic of the high standards of thirteenth-century architecture in the Seljuk capital. Haynes's vantage point once again fills the frame with the façade and minimises distortion*

40 *The Selim II Mosque and the Mevlana Lodge, Konya, seen
from the cemetery, 1884. Haynes contrasted the rough tombstones
with the elegant mosques and minarets behind them*

41 Konya's İnce Minareli Medrese (1258), seen from the citadel in 1884. Shooting from a high vantage point, Haynes isolated the medrese in the foreground, with the remains of the Zindankale fortress and the towers of the city walls beyond. The minaret from which the medrese took its name collapsed when it was struck by lightning in 1901

FOLLOWING PAGES
42 In this photograph of 1884, two girls stand before the portal of Konya's Sırçalı Medrese, built in 1242 by the tutor of the Seljuk Sultan Alaeddin Keykubad, Bedrettin Muslih, whose tomb lies next to the intricately sculpted entrance

43 A detail of the façade of the İnci Minareli Medrese, covered by a dizzying array of carved decoration, including intertwined bands of Koranic verse, 1884

SULTAN HAN

44 *The Sultan Han (1232–36), a caravanserai near Aksaray in central Anatolia, was part of the Seljuk development of transport routes along the Silk Road, providing secure overnight accommodation for travellers. Haynes photographed the ruins in 1884 and again in 1887. In this 1884 shot of the interior of the vaulted hall, looking north, Sterrett is standing in the background, next to the blocked entrance*

45 *The interior of the vaulted hall looking south, 1884. The high vantage point and dramatic recession compare with the 1881 Stillman/Haynes photograph of the Parthenon (plate 5)*

FOLLOWING PAGES
46 *The exterior of the portal of the Sultan Han's vaulted hall, covered by a 'muqarnas' (honeycomb) vault and framed by elaborate carving*
47 *The same portal seen from a distance. A figure posed next to the tower for a sense of scale appears minuscule. Both photographs were taken in 1884*

CAPPADOCIA

48 *Selime was Haynes's and Sterrett's first stop in the highlands of Cappadocia, in June 1884, marking their earliest encounter with the remarkable volcanic landscape and the rock-cut settlements of the so-called Troglodytes. Unable to sleep the first night, Haynes wrote, 'Altogether these rock formations and the multitude of excavated dwellings… appear to me now the most wonderful thing I have ever been permitted to rest my eyes upon in all my travels and among all the wonderfully interesting things it has been my good fortune to see in the land of wonders'*

49 *Sterrett and companions pause in a field north of Göreme, 1884. Behind
them an irregular row of volcanic cones, or 'fairy chimneys', is silhouetted
against the sky. Haynes took more than one hundred photographs of the strange
volcanic landforms of Cappadocia, the first photos of the region*

50 *Near Ürgüp in Cappadocia, 1884. Boulders that once formed the surface stratum appear precariously balanced on eroded volcanic cones. Haynes's photographs of the region were eventually published in 1919, in an article by Sterrett in The National Geographic Magazine entitled 'The Cone Dwellers of Asia Minor: A Primitive People Who Live in Nature-Made Apartment Houses Fashioned by Volcanic Violence and Trickling Streams'*

51 *About this photograph, taken either in 1884 or 1887, Haynes wrote: 'Several slender pinnacles at Utch Hissar in Cappodocia [sic], excavated into habitations by an unknown race of ancient people, the so-called Troglodytes'. Haynes was fascinated by the abstract character of the landscape in Cappadocia, particularly views that revealed almost no clues to human presence. Both he and Sterrett thought the rock-cut settlements were much older than the Byzantine period, and they ascribed the churches and chapels to the resettlement of the abandoned caves early in the Christian era*

52 *The entrance to a vaulted hall in a large, rock-cut mansion in Selime,*
probably from the eleventh century, with an elaborately carved lintel above
the door. When this 1884 photograph appeared in The National Geographic
Magazine in 1919, it was credited to Sterrett

53 *The interior of the church at Selime, 1884. In the panel below the lunette, seen from the west, is the poorly preserved eleventh-century fresco of the Virgin Mary with the donors and their family. Haynes took very few interior views of the rock-cut chambers. Before this photograph appeared in The National Geographic in 1919, it was retouched to make the figures more distinct*

54 *Avcılar (also called Maçan or Göreme village), Cappadocia, 1884. The façade of the Roman Tomb 10 has an arcaded vestibule. The tomb is now much eroded and enveloped by a new quarter of the town*

55   *The façade of the Bezirhane complex in Avcılar, much eroded in*
Haynes's 1884 photograph, has now completely fallen. The exposed,
barrel-vaulted vestibule opened to the hall of a small residential complex

56 *Çavuşin, Cappadocia. Haynes's photograph, taken in 1884 or 1887,*
shows the village before rockfall and collapse meant that it had to be
relocated. Towards the top of the village, the arcaded façade of the church of
John the Baptist appears partially preserved. Nothing now survives

57 *Göreme in 1884, long before the advent of tourism. The view of the monastic funerary area, now the Open Air Museum, looks south from the hill above Tokalı Kilise, where the modern road now passes*

58 *A view of the town of Uçhisar, surrounding the castle, 1884 or 1887.
A fascinating combination of rock-cut and built architecture, occupied
and abandoned, there is an almost hallucinatory quality to the settlement in
its Cappadocian landscape*

59 *A view of Uçhisar's castle and surrounding cones, 1884 or 1887.*
This was a favourite subject for Haynes in Cappadocia

60 *A residential area of Uçhisar, 1884 or 1887, displaying a characteristic mixture of masonry architecture and volcanic landforms*

61 *A Cappadocian landscape near Uçhisar, 1884 or 1887. The solid geometry
of the volcanic cones contrasts with the limited evidence of human presence.
In the foreground, the steps and vaulted entrance lead to an ancient tomb chamber*

62 *A view of the village of Avcılar from the north. Recently built houses fill the*
irregular spaces between the volcanic cones. In Roman times, this area was
a cemetery. The graininess of the print suggests that Haynes took the photograph
using a paper negative, a process with which he experimented on his 1887 journey.

63 *Ürgüp, a town of stone houses developed in the latter part of the nineteenth century along the base of the plateau. While intrigued by the mixture of masonry and rock-cut architecture, Haynes and Sterrett, who visited in 1884, found the inhabitants insufferable*

64 *The so-called Tomb of Hieron at Avcılar, 1884 or 1887. The rock-cut
funerary church, from the sixth or seventh century, has a carved façade, and
the floor of the interior is lined with tombs. Haynes and Sterrett both thought
the rock carvings were much older and attributed the churches and chapels
to Byzantine Christians fleeing Roman persecution. The regular carving
of the square façade and of the portal, with its neat horseshoe arch, contrasts
with the irregularly eroded landscape forms*

65 *Göreme, 1887. Steps lead through a fissure in the rock to a rock-cut*
chapel with a carved and painted façade, probably from the eleventh century

66 *The lack of both scale and human presence contributes to the abstract quality of this 1884 photograph of dovecotes in the cliffs at the entrance to the Soğanlı Valley*

67 The Roman mausoleum at Şar (Komana), seen from the southwest, as it appeared in 1884. One of the few examples of masonry architecture in Cappadocia, the monument survives in good condition. Haynes poses his travelling companions in the arches

KAYSERİ

68 *In 1884 and 1887 Haynes took several photographs of the cylindrical Sırçalı Kümbet, near the city of Kayseri in central Anatolia. Here, stepping away from the fourteenth-century Seljuk mausoleum, he maintains the alignment of the portals and creates a dramatic contrast between the solidity of the building and the frailty of the tombstones, filling one half of the frame with the dark monument, while leaving the other half open to empty air*

69 *In this close-up view of the Sırçalı Kümbet, Haynes aligns the portals to present a framed view into the landscape behind the mausoleum*

70 *Haynes chose this 1887 view of the mausoleum to publish in the 1892 folio; while providing more visual information than the previous two views, it is a less interesting composition*

BOĞAZKÖY

71 *A shrine at the Hittite capital of Hattusa, today's Boğazköy. The
Yazılıkaya, or 'inscribed stone', dates from 1250–1220 BC and depicts the
twelve gods of the underworld. Following Charles Texier's visit of 1834,
the site regularly attracted Western visitors*

Panorama of the walls of Angora   Hay Af. 150

72 *The walls of the Byzantine fortress at Ankara, 1884.*
As at Kayseri, Haynes contrasts the frail tombstones in the foreground
with the massive construction behind them

Pompeys pillar in Angora

Hay AC. 151

73 *The citadel of Ankara, 1884. At the time of Haynes's visit, Turkey's future capital
was no more than a small village amid the vestiges of antiquity. The Column of Julian
(which he called Pompey's Pillar) was erected to honour the Byzantine emperor's visit in 362*

74 *The entrance to Ankara's Temple of Augustus, dating from the
first century BC, with a fifteenth-century mosque, the Hacı Bayram Camii,
built against its flank and a cemetery in the foreground, 1884*

75 *The* Monumentum Ancyranum, *1884. The lateral façade of the Temple
of Augustus is inscribed with the text of the 'Res Gestae Divi Augusti', the
most complete surviving account of the deeds of Emperor Augustus, which was
added after his death in AD14*

76 *Arslan Tash (Turkish for 'Lion Stone'), the ancient site of Hadātu, in 1884. The man in the pith helmet posed like a big-game hunter next to an eighth-century BC Assyrian lion from the citadel gate is probably the Rev. Dr W. H. Ward, who led the Wolfe Expedition. Known to explorers as early as 1836, the site, now in northern Syria, was visited by the director of the Ottoman Imperial Museum, Osman Hamdi Bey, in 1885, but not until 1928 was it excavated by the French*

77 *General view of Arslan Tash, 1884, with one of the basalt lions fallen. William Hayes Ward noted that there were also fallen statues of bulls, which they were unable to photograph, blaming lack of co-operation by the locals*

78 *Another site known in modern times as Aslantaş, this one is near Darende, in southeast Turkey. The two stone lions are all that remain of a Hittite gate possibly dating from the twelfth or eleventh century BC. Explorers had discovered the site by 1858. In Haynes's 1884 photograph, a travelling companion poses on horseback, simulating the lions' stance*

79 *Zincirli, a Syro-Hittite citadel in the Anti-Taurus Mountains of south-central Turkey, was studied by Otto Puchstein in 1883 and later excavated by the Germans. Osman Hamdi Bey had encouraged the Americans to excavate the site, but they arrived too late. The carved stone blocks, or 'orthostats', lining the gateway of the citadel were found in their original position. Haynes used his gun for scale in this 1884 photograph*

80 *Marked by two Roman columns, the citadel of Urfa (modern Şanlıurfa)
in southeast Turkey offers a dramatic view over the city, 1884. According to
Muslim tradition, the columns were Nimrud's Throne. They are distinctive
for the lifting bosses left on the column drums. The Syriac inscription
indicates that Shalmet, the 'Son of the Sun', erected the columns for Queen
Eftuha in the early third century AD*

81 *Haynes's photograph of the ancient city of Harran, near Şanlıurfa, close to the modern border with Syria, 1884. Some of the traditional beehive houses with domes of mud brick survive to this day*

82　*The Wolfe Expedition's Armenian translator Daniel Z. Noorian seated amid the sculptures of Carchemish, 1885. When it was partially excavated by the British Museum in 1878–81, the inscriptions were removed, though the figural sculpture was left behind (a great pity, commented Ward). Part of a procession, the genie to the left holds a cone, flask and cloth for unction. To the right are the paws of a lion, mimicked by Noorian's gloved hands. The upper portion of the genie disappeared before excavations were resumed in 1911*

83 *A visitor, probably Ward, copying the inscription identifying the seated
figure as Bonus-tis, Queen of Carchemish, with the winged Naked Goddess
to the right, 1885. The broken panel was later reassembled by Sir Leonard
Woolley as a part of the long wall procession*

84 *Borsippa (Birs Nimrud), an ancient Sumerian city excavated by*
Sir Henry Cheswicke Rawlinson in 1854 and again by Hormuzd Rassam
for the British Museum between 1879 and 1881. The ziggurat, with
its distinctive tower, was identified in Talmudic and Arabic sources as the
Tower of Babel. Haynes visited the site with the Wolfe Expedition of 1885

85   *A view down the 'decumanus', or Grand Colonnade, of Palmyra, looking
north towards the Temple Tomb, 1885. On the distant hilltop is the medieval
castle, Qalaat Shirkuh. To the right are the ruins of the domestic quarter.
Haynes had been specifically requested by the AIA to photograph the caravan
city in the Syrian desert*

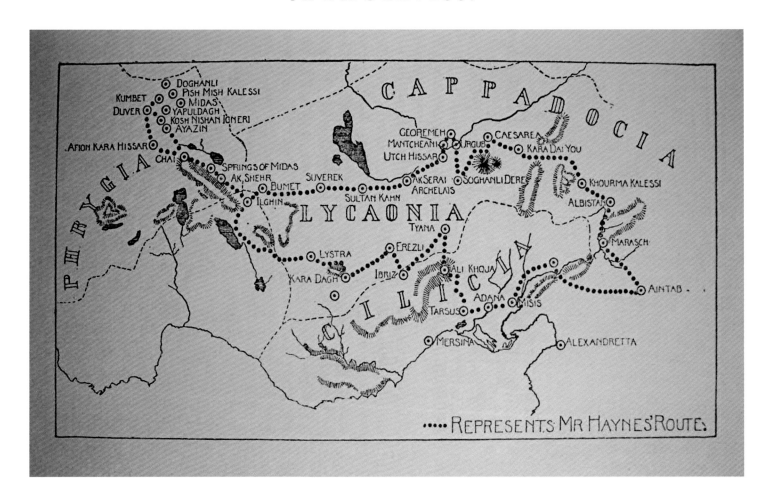

86 *Map showing Haynes's route for his 1887 journey across Anatolia.*
Published to accompany a folio of his photographs, the original is now preserved
in the archives of the American School of Classical Studies in Athens

87 *Haynes's 1892 folio begins with this record of a 'Hittite inscription on the
vertical face of a high cliff in the Taurus Mountains near the village of Ali
Khoja in the vicinity of the silver mines of Bulghar Dagh, some 20 miles N. W.
of the Cilician Gates in Cappadocia'. Near the modern village of Madenköy,
the hieroglyphic Luwian inscription dates from the eighth century BC. Although
Haynes provided no translation, the inscription is by the ruler Tarhunazas,
who received territory as a gift from King Warpalawas of Tyana*

88 *King Warpalawas prays to the Hurrian sky and storm god Teshup in this eighth-century BC neo-Hittite rock relief at Ivriz, near Konya. Haynes identified the figures as the god of harvest bearing fruits and anDura-Eoring priest. Building a scaffold in 1887 to photograph it, he noted that the god stands 13ft 11in tall*

89 *Church 8 of the isolated early Christian settlement of Binbirkilise ('the Thousand and One Churches'), southeast of Konya. William J. Hamilton's account of his visit in 1836–37 led other explorers to Binbirkilise. Haynes's 1887 photos are the oldest known from the site, which was devastated by an earthquake before Gertrude Bell and Sir William Ramsay studied it in 1907*

90 *Churches 13 and 8 at Binbirkilise, 1887. By the time Sir William Ramsay and Gertrude Bell documented the site, so little remained of Church 13 that they did not bother to record it. Haynes's two photographs provide our best record of it, showing the two-storey narthex and the foundations of the nave*

91 *In this study of the inner face of the narthex of Church 13, one of Haynes's companions is seen standing with a donkey in the foreground, while another crouches beneath a low arch on the opposite side of the building*

PHRYGIA

92 *The Arezastis Monument, near the village of Yazılı Kaya in the highlands of Phrygia, in western Anatolia, 1887. Already known to early travellers, this rock-cut façade, inscribed in the Phrygian language, is thought to date from c. 550 BC. Haynes may have been the first to photograph it*

93 *Haynes's 1887 photo is a unique record of Ayazin's Chamber Tomb 1. Sir William Ramsay, publishing it in 1882 (with incorrect drawings), regarded it as the most important chamber tomb carved under Greek influence. The pediment contained a gorgon's head, lions flanked the portal and figures appeared inside. The carving suffered much damage when the façade was later blocked by a barn*

94 *The monumental Gerdek Kaya, noted by early travellers in Phrygia, must belong to the Hellenistic period. It imitates a Doric 'in antis' building, with two tomb chambers behind and an arched sarcophagus niche carved into the rock below. In 1887 one column has fallen; the other hangs like a stalactite*

95 *Ayazin, Phrygia, 1887. This rock-cut Byzantine church – sometimes
erroneously called the Hamam – uniquely preserves its east façade, with
its carved apses, roofs and dome projecting from the cliff face. From its details
it can probably be dated to the late tenth or eleventh century*

QALAAT SAMAN

96 *Haynes and his companions camp in the courtyard of the fifth-century*
monastery of Qalaat Saman in Syria, c.1887. One of the great
pilgrimage shrines of the early Byzantine period, the monastery developed
around the site where the ascetic St Symeon Stylites spent forty years
sitting on top of a column in the Syrian Desert

97　*The monumental south façade of the great pilgrimage church of
St Symeon Stylites at Qalaat Saman, c.1887. Built to celebrate the saint's
spiritual triumph, the three-arched entry resembles a Roman triumphal arch*

98 *Qalaat Saman: the octagonal hall of the pilgrimage shrine, where once the column of the St Symeon stood, c.1887. By the late Middle Ages, pilgrims wishing to take home souvenirs of their visit had chipped the forty-foot column to a mere stub, which lay fallen amid the rubble when Haynes photographed the site*

BAGHDAD AND BEYOND

THE UNSUNG HERO OF NIPPUR

Unsettled, without financial means, and close to forty, Haynes had begun looking for a consular position, thinking that it might provide him better financial security and more free time for archaeological investigations. Norton and others intervened on his behalf, and for some time a consular posting in Beirut seemed a real possibility. Then in 1888 the Babylon Exploration Fund at the University of Pennsylvania launched an archaeological expedition to Mesopotamia, following on the recommendations of the Wolfe Expedition. They needed someone with on-the-ground experience to be their field manager and photographer. Ward steered them to Haynes, who gladly accepted the appointment. Moreover, as a part of the American strategy in the region, Haynes was named the first American consul in Baghdad in 1888, a position he held without salary until 1892, as he was on salary from the University of Pennsylvania. His luck seemed to be improving, although he had no idea of the discussions behind the scenes. To the Babylon Exploration Fund team he appeared 'a common, uneducated man'. John Punnett Peters (1852–1921), the team's leader, found him 'slow almost to exasperation', but supported him because he was 'faithful, honest, loyal, self-sacrificing & he knows how to manage the Turks & a caravan & to photograph'. As Haynes must have viewed this turn of events, he had finally gained recognition as an archaeologist; from the Babylon Exploration Fund's perspective, however, he was little more than a hired hand.

The Babylon Exploration Fund set its sights on Nuffar/Nippur, 180 kilometres south of Baghdad, one of the largest and most important cities of ancient Mesopotamia, sacred to the god Enlil. Located in the swamps of what is now southern Iraq, Nippur was difficult of access, inhospitable in its climate, surrounded by warring

99 *The Tigris at Baghdad photographed by Haynes when he first visited Baghdad with the Wolfe Expedition in 1885*

tribes, and not particularly attractive *(plates 102–114)*. All the same, the site offered tantalising clues to the early history of civilisation, and the Babylon Exploration Fund was lured by the prospect of a library of cuneiform tablets. But first the new antiquities laws and the person of Osman Hamdi Bey would have to be confronted.

In hindsight, the Americans appear unseasoned, naïve and presumptuous. Peters, the first expedition director *(plate 101)*, arrived in Constantinople in the summer of 1888 thinking that anything in the Imperial Museum was for sale; he was rebuffed. Then, not realising that Hamdi Bey was the author of the new antiquities legislation, Peters criticised it to his face. He did not make a favourable impression. His colleague and team member, the German-born Hermann Vollrath Hilprecht (1859–1925) *(plate 1c)*, fared much better, for he was both obsequious and European. Moreover, he arrived with an important bargaining chip – a rare understanding of Assyriology and cuneiform scripts that could be put to full advantage in setting up Hamdi Bey's new museum. Hilprecht would accordingly play an important part in the University of Pennsylvania's archaeological venture – and in Haynes's career as well.

As with Hamdi Bey, Hilprecht looms large in the story of Nippur. At the height of his fame, Hilprecht was called 'the Columbus of archaeology', although he actually spent very little time in the field. A talented but egotistical Assyriologist, he had studied in Germany before going to the U.S. in 1886, where he was appointed professor of Assyriology at the University of Pennsylvania. Tapped to participate in the expedition to Nippur, he declined at first because of his 'delicate health', but overcame his misgivings when he was appointed second-in-command to Peters. Understanding his peculiar combination of condescension, jealousy and hypochondria, the University of Pennsylvania provost, William Pepper, commented, 'Hilprecht will die if he does go, and he will die if he does not.' Hilprecht went, but he complained all the way: about the Oriental paupers, the vermin, the travel conditions that were 'beneath my dignity and that of the University', but mostly about his colleagues.

The first expedition was delayed in Constantinople waiting for the excavation permit, and the team did not arrive in Baghdad until January 1889, whence they headed downriver to Nippur. By mid-April, however, the expedition had terminated calamitously. The team had found barely enough to justify continuing, and the season was marred by infighting. While there were many large egos in the group, the participants were singularly united by their hatred of the tyrannical Peters, who in spite of his complete lack of archaeological experience demanded complete authority in all decisions. Hilprecht called him 'demonic'. Mutiny threatened at almost every turn. Their difficulties were exacerbated by the enmity of the locals, who robbed them and burned their camp as they departed, culminating in mass resignations.

Hilprecht did not resign, but simply refused to go back to the site, allegedly to save the Babylon Exploration Fund money. Ingeniously he arranged to position himself in Constantinople, at the university's

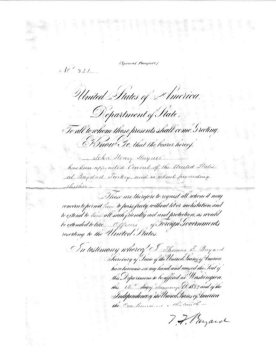

100 *Haynes served as the first American consul in Baghdad, 1888–92*

expense, to maintain good relations with the Ottoman authorities and to negotiate the division of the finds. Because Ottoman laws did not allow for the export of antiquities, foreign excavators were at the mercy of the Ottoman authorities to give them part of their finds as 'gifts', a practice Hilprecht used to his advantage. As he later insisted, the antiquities from Nippur destined for the University of Pennsylvania had been given to him 'as personal gifts of the Sultan', most of which he then magnanimously donated to the university.

Only Haynes, who had remained as consul in Baghdad, and a reluctant Peters returned for a second, more successful season (1889–90), when 8,000 tablets were found. But the conditions were too much for Peters. After two seasons, he begged off and set himself to write a two-volume account of the expedition. The University of Pennsylvania found itself without a director for an expedition in which it had invested time, money and its reputation. The university's prestige was at stake. While the Babylon Exploration

Fund held out hope of great discoveries, both Peters and Hilprecht were happier in the library than in the field. Both wanted to take credit for the results of the expedition, but neither was willing to return to the site. And although he goes almost unmentioned, the Wolfe Expedition's translator, Noorian, who had returned for the first two seasons at Nippur, also chose not to continue. When asked about a third season, Peters's response to the Babylon Exploration Fund was short and to the point: 'Impossible! Let Haynes go it alone.' Seeing no alternative, they agreed. Haynes thus returned alone for a long third season (1893–96), accompanied only by a local servant and another translator.

Haynes remained willing, but he simply did not have the proper background to take charge. While the Babylon Exploration Fund recognised his shortcomings, they also valued his dependability, and on the basis of the latter they believed he could be directed from afar. This turned out to be more difficult than any of them imagined. Letters between Philadelphia and Nippur took weeks to reach their destination, so that instructions were usually out of date even before they were dispatched and pointless by the time they arrived. Overseeing a large team of workmen drawn from feuding tribes, while documenting the excavations, communicating regularly with Philadelphia and taking photographs under adverse conditions – with temperatures often above 100 degrees Fahrenheit – Haynes was rapidly overwhelmed. It is hard to imagine his state of mind during this period. Why did he agree to continue alone on an expedition that (at least in hindsight) seemed cursed from the beginning? Was it simply his lack of finances or lack of opportunities elsewhere, or did he hold out hope of archaeological success, even fame? Whatever his motivation, his depression gradually turned to paranoia. Haynes constantly feared for his life but found little sympathy from Peters in Philadelphia, who criticised his insufficient excavation reports and instructed him that 'the Committee want tablets'. His repeated requests for assistants at the site went unanswered.

In the reports from the Babylon Exploration Fund from this time, Haynes appears infuriatingly slow and dull-witted. To be fair, he was out of his element and in over his head. His previous archaeological experience at Assos gave him little preparation for the challenges of Mesopotamia: it is much easier to distinguish stone ashlar or marble from dirt than it is to differentiate mud from mud brick. He knew the

101 *Osman Hamdi Bey, the renowned Ottoman statesman, archaeologist and painter who founded the Ottoman Imperial Museum, with John Punnett Peters (standing), first scientific director of the University of Pennsylvania's mission to Nippur, 1889. Although the two did not see eye to eye, Hamdi Bey supported the Americans' archaeological venture and awarded them the permit to excavate at Nippur (Photographer unknown)*

rudiments of ancient Greek, enough at least to have a sense of the worth of an inscription when one was uncovered at Assos. He was familiar with Greek civilisation, its religion, its aesthetics, its architecture. At Nippur, everything was unfamiliar. He had only a vague sense of the nature of Sumerian civilisation, its belief system and its architecture. Most critically, its written languages were unknown to him, its cuneiform script impossible for him to decipher. At Assos he had been part of a team; now, at Nippur, he was alone.

Charged with finding cuneiform tablets, he had no way to determine the potential value of those he unearthed. And while the Babylon Exploration Fund's first interest was to recover the literary record, their instructions to Haynes about excavating were vague at best. Peters, no archaeologist himself, had established a crude method of random, predatory tunnelling – that is, treasure-hunting rather than systematic archaeology – that Haynes was obliged to follow. As an archaeologist he recognised the problematic and destructive nature of their explorations, for which he apologised in a later report, but all major decisions were made by others, off-site.

During the summer of 1894, stranded by floods during a trip to Baghdad, Haynes met by chance a recent Massachusetts Institute of Technology architecture graduate, Joseph A. Meyer (1856–94), whom he induced to join the expedition. A talented and artistic young man, Meyer was on a travelling scholarship from MIT to study world architecture. His insight and graphic skills made significant contributions in clarifying the architecture and urban landscape at Nippur (plate 111). More importantly, he provided Haynes with companionship in his 'lonely and desolate life'. The two formed a strong emotional bond, and Haynes's spirits and work both improved dramatically.

Less than six months later, however, Meyer was dead from dysentery. It had been a protracted and painful death, and Haynes felt both a terrible responsibility and a profound sense of loss. His mental condition rapidly deteriorated once more. He seems to have had a mental breakdown, but insisted on soldiering on. By the time the Babylon Exploration Fund was finally able to send assistance, in the spring of 1896, more than a year after Meyer's death, Haynes was convinced of imminent danger and insisted on immediate evacuation, to the embarrassment – financial and otherwise – of the university.

Haynes returned to the United States for a period of rest and recuperation. Pushed by the Babylon Exploration Fund, he hastily prepared an account of the excavations for publication, but it never saw the light of day. Jealous of the successful publication by Peters, Hilprecht intervened, stopped the printing, then insisted on editing the manuscript himself. The project was never completed. As it survives in typescript, the report is vague, rambling and disorganised. Still, Haynes emerged in a far more positive light following his long season of hardships. There were significant finds, his photographs were impressive, and he had demonstrated the financial viability of year-round excavation. The University of Pennsylvania, perhaps

to appear supportive, awarded him an honorary BSc in 1895. He received a master's degree from his alma mater, Williams, at the same time, followed by an honorary Doctor of Science degree in 1896. In the same year, according to his family, Robert College conferred a PhD on him, but there is no record of this. Unfortunately Haynes's activities during this period are not easy to follow. When he was not travelling abroad, he did not keep a diary.

With the Babylon Exploration Fund's blessing, Haynes returned to direct the fourth and final season at Nippur (1898–1900), but during his time in the United States, to the surprise of everyone, he got married. Taciturn and close to fifty, he met the ebullient Cassandria Artella Smith during a visit to the Smithsonian, and he married her shortly thereafter, in March 1897. Little is known of her life. Thirteen years his junior, she came from Ottawa, Illinois, by way of Chicago, and had been previously married. To the consternation of the fund's officers, Haynes insisted that she accompany him to Nippur (plate 112). While Haynes was no great catch, his family regarded Cassandria as a floozy and a gold-digger.

The mudflats of southern Mesopotamia proved not to be the Garden of Eden, and their relationship quickly deteriorated during the long, harsh months at Nippur. They separated soon after the end of the excavation. Adding to the tensions, Haynes's young assistants, Clarence Fisher and Valentine Geere, arrived more than eight months late. Geere had been laid low in Baghdad with 'pleur-pneumonia' and had been left in the care of the American consul; Fisher stayed behind to tend the invalid Geere, then for reasons unexplained retreated to London, after which he returned to accompany Geere to Nippur. To complicate matters – perhaps the explanation for his indecisiveness – Fisher had developed a hopeless, unrequited infatuation with Geere: he wrote poetry to him, had been observed kissing him, and regularly threatened to kill himself if his sentiments were not reciprocated. The atmosphere at the dig house began to resemble Who's Afraid of Virginia Woolf?

In his memoirs, Geere portrays Haynes as an incompetent bungler and a pedant, and Cassandria as a shrew with an infernal temper. When Fisher and Geere arrived, they found the two already pitted against each other, but quickly realised that the Hayneses could direct their hostilities against the two young men as well. Haynes struggled to maintain a balance, keeping the peace with his wife while overseeing the progress of the excavation, and he had difficulties with both. His lack of leadership was met with sloth and insouciance by Geere and Fisher, who often slept in and spent their days playing chess rather than attending to the excavation. Still, Cassandria kept the dig house in order, presided over their daily dinners, and as Haynes's secretary she wrote reports on the daily excavation activities, at least as she understood them.

More importantly, in the final season of digging, Haynes hit the mother lode: in early 1900 he unearthed what was alleged to be the Temple Library, from which 23,000 tablets were extracted. It was a major discovery, and although we now know the site to be the scribal quarter and not the library, much of what we know of the ancient Sumerian literary tradition comes as the result of Haynes's discovery. While no one on site was capable of understanding the true nature of the find, all recognised its significance. Haynes's years of perseverance as an archaeologist had finally paid off.

Haynes's glory was short-lived, however. In March 1900, Hilprecht returned to Nippur after eleven years' absence and immediately took charge. By that time, most of the work was finished, and the tablets had been crated for shipment. Hilprecht spent a mere ten weeks at the site, attempting to put in order what had been directed from afar for the previous decade, complaining and criticising all the way. His account of the situation at the excavation was scathing: as he saw it, the Americans had simply torn up the site. Haynes, he wrote, should have known better. Claiming to have personally rescued the expedition, he publicly took credit for Haynes's discoveries, dismissed Haynes as incompetent, his wife as a 'bad influence', and his assistants as 'cocksuckers' – the last in his private diary, in German. Hilprecht returned home a famous man; newspapers wrote of his heroism leading dangerous expeditions for the past decade and of his sensational finds. The University of Pennsylvania rewarded him with a medal, a research professorship, and a three-year paid leave to catalogue the tablets and to conduct research in Constantinople.

Haynes came away from the discovery of a lifetime empty-handed. His career in a shambles, his marriage disintegrating, his health failing, he retreated to upstate Massachusetts and disappeared from public view. We have no good record of his final decade. Haynes had arranged for his servant Mustafa to emigrate to the United States,

but it is unclear what became of him. Haynes had a second mental breakdown and by 1905 was institutionalised. Cassandria, who no longer lived with him, lectured to women's groups about her travails in Mesopotamia; she died in 1906. Haynes worked briefly for the Internal Revenue Service in California – as his family recalled, after so many years in Mesopotamia, he found the winters of New England too cold for comfort. At the end of his life, however, he was back in Massachusetts, living with his sister Hannah and her husband, Charles S. Peach, in North Adams. He died 'Broken in Body and Spirit', as his obituary read in the *North Adams Evening Transcript* of June 29, 1910, unrecognised for his many accomplishments. Only on his deathbed did he break his decade-long silence on the Nippur excavations, giving a lengthy interview to the *Transcript* about the true nature of the discoveries and his role in them.

While Haynes faded from view, Hilprecht's star was on the rise, but his mistreatment of Haynes did not go unnoticed and was not forgotten. With the publication of his *Explorations in Bible Lands During the 19th Century* in 1903, public opinion of the scholar began to shift. In the book, Hilprecht overplayed his hand, touting the University of Pennsylvania's accomplishments at Nippur above all previous discoveries and scholarship in Mesopotamia. At the same time, he deprecated the contributions of Haynes and Peters and ignored all other members of the expedition; its success was to be credited to him alone. To add insult to injury, numerous uncredited photographs by Haynes were used to illustrate the book, including its magnificent and evocative frontispiece *(plate 106)*, taken in 1893, when Hilprecht was nowhere near the site. As Hilprecht's critics hastened to note, Haynes, and not he, had discovered the Temple Library; moreover, his claims as to the contents and significance of the library could not be substantiated; the tablets were still in crates, unexamined, at the University of Pennsylvania Museum. More damning was the realisation that many of the tablets used as illustrations in his book were not from Nippur at all: they either came from elsewhere or had been purchased in the Baghdad bazaar. Even more embarrassingly, some of the artefacts from the excavation never made it to the museum, ending up as Hilprecht's private property.

John Punnett Peters was Hilprecht's most vocal critic. Hilprecht had replaced him as scientific director, and the two men had loathed each other since their falling-out during the first season at Nippur. In

102 *The mounds at Nippur, 1893. The site of the ancient Sumerian city, in what is now southern Iraq, was enormous, and early excavation techniques were not very sophisticated. In the foreground, workers dump earth removed from the temple court; in the background the mounds are scarred by deep trenches dug by the University of Pennsylvania team in search of cuneiform tablets*

March 1905, at Peters's insistence, the University of Pennsylvania launched a formal inquiry that became known as 'the Peters–Hilprecht Controversy'. As his behaviour of the past years had amply demonstrated, Hilprecht's ego had got the better of him. His relations with Assyriologist colleagues and students had frayed; they were more than happy to testify against him. Sadly, Haynes was declared too 'mentally unbalanced' to testify on his own behalf, as a note from the sanatorium doctor explained; he was represented at the proceedings by the estranged Cassandria. In the end, the University of Pennsylvania's trustees found the charge of 'literary dishonesty' unsubstantiated. Feeling himself vindicated, Hilprecht published an edited transcript of the hearings, but doubts still lingered. His critics were not satisfied.

Hilprecht ultimately found himself on the wrong side of the university. When questions arose surrounding his care of the Temple Library tablets in 1910, he abruptly departed for Europe, taking the keys to the storerooms with him. The director of the museum changed the locks and investigated, finding the tablets deteriorating in their packing crates and no record as to where they had been found. Hilprecht had been too busy travelling, lecturing and basking in glory to attend to the discovery on which his fame rested. Accused of negligence, he resigned in protest, and to his great surprise, the trustees accepted his resignation. Hilprecht returned to Jena in Germany, but to all intents and purposes his professional career ended in 1910, shortly after Haynes's death. Osman Hamdi Bey passed away in the same year. It was the end of an era.

On December 5, 1913, in a ceremony attended by family, friends and scholars, a monument was unveiled at Haynes's grave, a replica of the Black Obelisk of the Assyrian king Shalmaneser III. On its face is a relief of the ziggurat from Nippur and the name of the tomb's occupant, John Henry Haynes, identified simply as 'Archaeological Explorer' *(plate 116)*. His birth date was recorded incorrectly; his photography was not mentioned.

103 *The excavation headquarters at Nippur, 1892. In the first two seasons, life at Nippur was relatively primitive, as the site was little more than a fortified compound of tents and huts, seen here against the backdrop of southern Mesopotamia's seemingly endless mudflats*

104 *Settling in for the long third 'season', 1893–96, in what he called 'Robberdom and Murderland', Haynes had a proper (and secure) dig house constructed, known as 'the Castle'. The traditional mud-brick house, or 'meftûl', was located at the southern foot of the ruins, surrounded by gardens and reed huts and eventually equipped with its own water supply. It served as the residence and headquarters of the team for the remainder of the excavation*

105 *Excavation of the temple courtyard at Nippur, c.1894.*
Haynes's photograph emphasises the immensity of the enterprise
against the vastness of the surrounding plain

106 *Taken in 1893 during the long third excavation (1893–96), this view of the temple courtyard gives a sense of the scale of the dig, for which Haynes was the sole archaeologist on site. The most interesting features, such as the towers and stairs, are by-products of the excavation and were later removed.*

Nevertheless, the Assyriologist Hilprecht chose this photograph for the frontispiece of his infamous 1903 book, 'Explorations in Bible Lands'. His friend Osman Hamdi Bey based an enormous oil painting on the frontispiece image. In neither case did Haynes receive a credit

107 *The temple courtyard, c.1894. Haynes captures the atmosphere of the site in a dramatic image of contrasting darks and lights. Like an army of ants, workers toil up the steps*

108 *Excavation of a drain at Nippur, 1893 or 1894. In a carefully composed photograph, Haynes poses a worker so that the angle of his body mirrors that of the ceramic pipes behind him*

109 *In a similar way to his early photographs at Assos, Haynes poses a local boy next to a brick arch so that the triangle of his body mimics that of the arch, 1893 or 1894*

NIPPUR
NORTH-WEST FAÇADE
of the ZIGGURAT.
EXCAVATED DURING the
SUMMER of 1894.

SHEET Nº 26

110 For this 1894 photograph of the base of Nippur's ziggurat, Haynes chose a high vantage point and an angle that emphasises spatial recession, with a lone workman standing on top of the platform

111 The northwest façade of the ziggurat, by Joseph A. Meyer, 1894. The MIT architecture graduate spent less than six months at the excavations before dying from dysentery. His remarkable sketches and renderings reveal the scale and significance of the site's architectural remains. Meyer worked from pencil sketches done on site to produce impressive ink drawings like this one. Like Haynes, he favoured high vantage points, dramatic angles and isolated figures

112 *A local celebration at Nippur, 1899 or 1900. Carried aloft by workers and shaded by an umbrella, Haynes's wife, Cassandria, appears to be enjoying herself. Taciturn and nearly fifty, Haynes had met and married the younger Cassandria in 1897. She accompanied him for the fourth and final season of excavation. The marriage did not last, and Mrs Haynes later gave talks to women's groups about her travails in Mesopotamia*

113 *A party from Nippur returns home by boat along a channel of the
Euphrates, after a visit to a local chieftain, 1899 or 1900. In the final season
at Nippur, Haynes became increasingly interested in the lives of the local tribes,
and his photographs provide a valuable anthropological record*

114 *Camel herds of the powerful Shammar tribe grazing on the plains near Nippur, 1899 or 1900. In Haynes's day, the ancient city was surrounded by warring tribes*

AN EYE FOR THE PICTURESQUE

The Photographer as Artist

John Henry Haynes's career as a photographer began in Athens in 1881, working as the assistant to William J. Stillman *(plate 1B)*. Stillman was the singular formative influence on his craft. While coming from humble beginnings similar to those of Haynes, Stillman was his polar opposite – social and outgoing rather than shy and private, a man of many words, more capricious than dependable. After graduating from Union College in upstate New York in 1848, Stillman began his career as a painter, studying landscape painting briefly with Frederic Church. Stillman subsequently discovered John Ruskin's book *Modern Painters* (1843), which he later claimed had changed his life; he received from it 'a stimulus to nature worship… which made ineffaceable the confusion in my mind between nature and art'. In 1849 he sold his first painting and used the proceeds to book a passage to England, ostensibly to see the works of J.M.W. Turner, who was championed by Ruskin. Through an odd combination of coincidence, personal charm and determination, he was able to meet both Turner and Ruskin at that time. Travelling to Paris the following year, he met many of the active painters and developed a special relationship with Théodore Rousseau, whom he regarded as the greatest of the French landscape painters.

Back in America in 1855, he founded the art journal *The Crayon*, in which he advocated the art theory of Ruskin. Stillman was able to convince major figures, including Ruskin, to contribute their writings to it. Following Ruskin's model, Stillman wrote regular essays on the transcendent importance of Art (with a capital A) to human society. Although short-lived, the journal introduced Ruskin's principles to the American public. And by means of the journal, Stillman connected with the intellectual circles of Boston and Cambridge, primarily through the figure of James Russell Lowell. Under the name the Adirondack Club or the Philosophers' Club, he organised wilderness outings for them, during which they could discuss art, aesthetics, nature and philosophy in rustic surroundings. Then, while recovering from a bout of pneumonia in Florida, Stillman acquired a camera and took up photography. His earliest efforts, evocative views of the dense Adirondack woods, were published in 1859.

The following year, he left his fiancée behind in Cambridge and returned to England. There he befriended the circle of Pre-Raphaelite artists, who were also favourites of Ruskin. He subsequently became known as 'the American Pre-Raphaelite', perhaps more for his melodramatic lifestyle than for his artistic ability. He also became a companion and protégé of Ruskin, with whom he travelled to Switzerland in 1860.

They eventually fell out when Stillman made the mistake of asking Ruskin's opinion of his paintings. Met with muted enthusiasm, Stillman destroyed his remaining canvases, suffered an episode of hysterical blindness, then renounced painting in favour of photography, archaeology and eventually journalism. The rift was healed and, following his marriage, he named his first child John Ruskin Stillman (aka Russie) after his mentor. Although he had lost confidence in his own talent as a painter and sought other employment, he continued to champion Ruskin's art. He served briefly as American consul in Rome, then as consul in Crete. At neither was he successful, for Stillman tended to become personally involved in local causes – support of the Greek insurrection in Crete was just one of many political mistakes in his career. Moreover, the constant dislocation and financial insecurity proved too much for his wife, who committed suicide in Athens in 1868, shortly after they had fled Crete. Left in financial straits with three small children and Russie showing the first signs of a debilitating illness that would eventually kill him, Stillman returned to photography. Possibly his greatest professional and artistic success was the folio of photographs of the Athenian Acropolis, prepared in 1869 and issued in 1870.

The album's photographs are stunningly original, with daring angles and recession into space, dramatic contrasts of dark and light, and unusual vantage points, creatively bringing together a Ruskinian sense of aesthetics and a more scholarly approach to architectural form *(plates 2–4)*. The title of the folio summarises Stillman's approach: *The Acropolis of Athens: Illustrated Picturesquely and Architecturally in Photography.* The key words, of course, are picturesquely and architecturally. While focusing on the delineation of structural form, he nevertheless introduces all the aesthetic sensibilities of the picturesque as defined by Ruskin, as well as drawing on his previous experience as a painter of landscapes.

In some of the views, he pulls away from his subject, isolating it in the surrounding landscape, while giving equal emphasis to foreground, middle ground and background. In still others, he frames the subject close at hand in intimate views. Broken lines and the contrasts of light and shadow fill out his toolbox of Ruskinian details. His views are as modern as the Turner landscapes he had admired a decade earlier. A final detail adds to the modernity of his photographs – the regular inclusion of the modern population in his views, in accord with his philhellenic sentiments.

These are neither touristic views nor simply landscapes with ruins, but carefully analysed studies of antiquities seen in their contemporary setting. They represent a summation of everything Stillman had learnt, contemplated and reassessed throughout the previous decade from the writings of Ruskin, as well as from the photographer's many personal encounters with him.

Stillman returned to London in 1870, renewed his acquaintance with the Pre-Raphaelites, and met and married the painter and artists' muse Marie Spartali. For much of his later life he worked as a journalist. In 1874 he published *Poetic Localities of Cambridge*, with his photographs accompanied by texts written by his old friends from the Adirondack Club. When the newly founded Archaeological Institute of America became interested in the possibility of an excavation in Crete, Stillman appeared to have the necessary experience to lead the expedition. Unfortunately, his previous political involvement was taken into consideration only too late. Thus, in 1881, Stillman found himself at a loose end in Athens, with John Henry Haynes in tow.

What to do? Stillman decided to use the opportunity to redo his 1870 folio, his greatest professional success. This would serve as Haynes's apprenticeship in the art of photography. Rather than launch into something new, Stillman monomaniacally attempted to re-create the original folio. More than a decade had passed since its publication, but it still appeared stunningly original. For each new photograph, he sought to replicate the exact framing, vantage points and camera angles of the original *(compare plates 4 and 5)*, with Haynes at his elbow as he no doubt explained the visual effect he was seeking. Stillman's dogged determination to find exactly the right view, properly framed, must have impressed Haynes, and the short apprenticeship had a lasting impact on Haynes's own photography.

Although his personality was much more subdued than that of his teacher, Haynes's compositions are often remarkably similar. For example, the dramatic angles, high vantage point and spatial recession in Haynes's interior photos of the Sultan Han seem to echo those employed by Stillman at the Parthenon *(compare plates 4 and 45)*. The calculated isolation of monuments and figures within the landscape is also comparable: Haynes's views of Eflatunpınar compare nicely with Stillman's views of Athens *(compare plates 2 and 34)*. So, too, Haynes's striking contrasts of solids and voids match Stillman's: Haynes's view of the massive *türbe*, or mausoleum, at Kayseri set against frail tombstones with a view into limitless space may be seen side by side with Stillman's view of the Parthenon stylobate *(compare plates 3 and 68)*. In fact, several views of Athens once in Haynes's possession correspond to published photographs by Stillman; they are unlabelled and could easily be the work of either man *(see plate 5)*. As with Stillman's views, there is always an element of compositional artistry in Haynes's work. From his short apprenticeship, Haynes rapidly developed the discerning eye of a picturesque landscape painter combined with a profound understanding of Ruskinian aesthetics.

What is most astonishing is that what Stillman had nurtured and developed as an intellectual and aesthete over the course of a decade Haynes seems to have picked up instinctively with less than two months of informal instruction. While perhaps indicative of the differences of personality between the two men, it remains unclear how much (or how little) Haynes knew about Ruskinian aesthetics per se. The great critic is nowhere mentioned in Haynes's voluminous correspondence and diaries. Nor is the term picturesque (at least in the Ruskinian sense), and one wonders if Haynes fully comprehended his own artistic abilities – or even if he regarded his photographs as art.

Although by his own admission Haynes struggled with the technical aspects of printing and developing, his images are remarkably sophisticated in composition. Indeed, Haynes continued to write about the types of plates and their preparation, printing techniques, acquisition of the necessary chemicals and papers, and the like, and yet he never once explained how he composed a photograph. Art (with a capital A) never entered his discussion. Still, Haynes's archaeological photography at Assos in 1882 and 1883 reflects the direct application of Stillman's teachings and indicates just how much he had learnt. Basic formal principles learnt from Stillman are reflected: distant views of the hill and the acropolis, for example, seem to follow the formal organisation of Stillman's Athenian photography, with the outcropping isolated in the distance and other features appearing in the near and middle grounds *(plates 7 and 8)*. In one odd view, he had Sterrett sitting in the roadway for no apparent reason, as another abstract form in a composition of opposing darks and lights; the acropolis of Assos appears almost as an afterthought in the distance.

Like Stillman, Haynes often favoured high vantage points, dramatic angles and spatial recession. The topography of Assos lent itself to these views. Haynes photographed the harbour dramatically from the city above *(plate 6)*; the steeply pitched theatre appears at a striking angle, as do views of the agora, its walls and steps forming parallel lines that recede into the distance *(plate 9)*. Similarly, the views of the walls of the ancient city are carefully studied. Details of the gateways, for example, are often seen from above and at an angle, usually with one of the workers or an archaeologist posed for scale and offering a second focus to the composition *(plate 10)*.

Evidence of modern life continues to sneak into the pictures as well. Distant views show the village of Behram set at the base of the acropolis and the settlement at the harbour below. Rather than isolate the ruins, Haynes depicted them in their contemporary setting. He regularly employed one of the village boys, who appear almost as an alternative subject in many of his archaeological views. In one photograph, ostensibly a study of wall-construction techniques, a boy appears smiling, front and centre, slouching against the wall *(plate 11)*. Which is more important, the wall or the boy? In another, a boy – perhaps the same one – seated on an ancient bench turns to peer coyly round the corner, as a late afternoon shadow creeps across the lower steps *(plate 12)*. In yet another, a lone horseman appears nobly silhouetted against the sky on an ancient Ottoman bridge *(plate 13)*. The message behind the photographs, as with so many of Stillman's from Athens, is that the remains of Assos may be ancient, but the inhabitants are modern. Like Stillman, Haynes extended the historical experience into the present.

In several of the excavation photographs, Haynes juxtaposed workers and remains in amusing, sometimes mimetic ways. For a view of a rock-cut anthropomorphic tomb, he posed a worker beside it, seated with an umbrella, mimicking the round shape at the head of the tomb *(plate 14)*. In addition, the umbrella offers a point of stark contrast in a sunlit view. Indeed, while the tomb of the dead is brilliantly lit, the umbrella casts a dark shadow across the single living being in the photograph. In another view, a barefoot boy sits cross-legged on top of a capital from the temple, his dirty foot casting a shadow over it *(plate 15)*; in another, a worker of distinctly non-Classical proportions poses uncomfortably on top of an inscribed statue base *(plate 16)*. Not simply appearing for scale, the figures offer a second point of focus in each view and serve to situate the antiquities within the context of the present. These and other of Haynes's best photos from Assos introduce contemporary life into the ancient remains. The workers engage with the ancient city, just as Stillman's modern Athenians had done. When seen at work, there is a sense of nobility to their enterprise – another element that might be derived indirectly from Ruskin's teachings *(plates 9 and 17)*. Moreover, like Stillman, Haynes was a philhellene; the contemporary ethnic Greeks are set in the context of their own cultural history, as the rightful inheritors of a glorious past. While Clarke and Bacon might have been engrossed in the politics and economics of archaeology – that is, claiming their share of loot for the sponsors in Boston – Haynes's photographs suggest a different agenda, a concern for heritage and cultural identity.

How the archaeologists are portrayed is also significant. Unlike the grand travel photographs of an earlier generation, in which Westerners appear as colonial conquerors, actively capturing or possessing the past, Haynes's archaeologists appear more passive. Because of the necessary exposure time, the peopled views had to be carefully staged, but only rarely is action suggested. More often the archaeologists are set in contemplative poses: rather than manual labour they engage in more intellectual pursuits. They are archaeologists 'doing' archaeology – that is, scholars rather than conquerors, interpreting the past as they uncover it *(plates 18 and 19)*.

Haynes occasionally managed to bring a sense of life into his photographs of the small finds as well. In one, a Pergamene pilaster capital forms the pedestal for fragments of three portrait heads of different periods. Turning towards each other, they appear as if participating in a lively conversation *(plate 20)*. Something is going on here, the photograph tells us; there's a story here somewhere.

In another shot, Haynes puts together three small ceramic figurines, seating them on the edge of a book, shown in close-up *(plate 21)*. Undisguised, the book introduces both scale and an element of modernity into the view; the three figurines appear seated like charming dolls at a tea party. The viewer is struck both by the intimacy of the shot and by the potential for narrative.

Haynes brought many of the same themes to the photographs he took during his Anatolian travels of 1884 and 1887. For example, at Eflatunpınar, a Hittite site near Lake Beyşehir dating from c.1300 BC, he pulls away from the Hittite monument,

isolating it against the barren landscape, while his fellow travellers set up camp at the water's edge in front of the spring *(plate 33)*. The pale solids of the tenting contrast with the sculpted details of the monument: the travellers' transitory presence is juxtaposed against the immutable permanence of the monument, the softness of cloth against the hardness of stone. Pack animals graze, tended by their keepers, a companion rests, almost unnoticed behind them. Crates and equipment are scattered about. As at Assos, we view the archaeologist 'doing' archaeology – or perhaps more correctly, the photographer 'doing' photography. The intrusive modernity of Haynes's scientific venture becomes the subtext in the recording of antiquity. In a detailed photograph of the monumental façade, one of Haynes's travelling companions leans against its flank, his discomfort evident as he poses ankle-deep in the frigid spring *(plate 34)*. Joining the line-up of the gods of earth and sky carved on the façade, his transience contrasts with their monolithic permanence.

A scene of the late-fifth-century pilgrimage shrine of Qalaat Saman in northern Syria is similar, setting the brevity of human experience against the timeless, monumental grandeur of the archaeological remains. Haynes's encampment appears in the courtyard of the ruined monastery, enveloped by pillared porticoes *(plate 96)*. The mules graze while the team rests on the fallen stones. Compared to the architecture they appear inconsequential, even trivial. At first glance, other photographs from Qalaat Saman offer bleak vistas of monumental architecture long since abandoned *(plates 97 and 98)*. But a second look reveals within the stillness and isolation an inevitable human presence. Men stand to the side, hide in the shadows, crouch in the distance. The so-called 'Dead Cities' come to life before Haynes's lens. All provide evidence of Haynes's subjective engagement with the past. Only in detailed views is the human presence missing.

At Konya Haynes found an entirely different period of historic architecture, primarily that of the thirteenth-century Seljuks, for whom Konya functioned as the capital. There he repeatedly photographed the complex of the Alaeddin Camii, the throne mosque for the Seljuk Sultans of Rum (Anatolia), which contained their dynastic mausolea, and which was built in stages in the twelfth and thirteenth centuries *(plates 36–38)*. In one view, seen from the north, he includes the Seljuk kiosk, once part of the palace and since disappeared; the area in between is filled with ruins that once formed part of the palace. In another view, seen from the east, he pulls away from the complex, emphasising the isolation and sense of abandonment. The rise of the terrain combines with the recession into space to provide a sense of scale. Jagged lines form a rough zigzag, leading the eye into the picture space, while the architecture appears as contrasts of textures. Haynes took several details of the mosque as well, notably of the north façade, where the elegantly carved and polychrome stone ornament contrasts with evidence of decay and abandonment, such as the lavishly framed but rudely blocked portal *(plate 38)*. Throughout one sees Byzantine spolia, such as the many reused window mullions, of several different sizes, set sideways to frame the Seljuk arched window openings. Through Haynes's lens, the contrasting textures of building materials construct a historical narrative.

Almost no people appear in Haynes's photographs of Konya – the mosques and their details are isolated and impersonal. The close-up of the Sahip Ata Camii (1285) concentrates on the sophisticated geometric ornamentation of the façade, while the view is closed off by rude walls to either side *(plate 39)*. What looks like a dark figure huddled at the entrance on closer inspection turns out to be a large ceramic vessel. The cemetery by the shrine of Rumi is similarly deserted, untended and overgrown with weeds, its irregular tombstones allowing a study of textures *(plate 40)*. Most dramatic of the Konya views is the panorama of the İnce Minareli Medrese (built 1258), isolated against the landscape, viewed from the mound at the centre of town on which the Alaeddin Camii sits *(plate 41)*. In the distance are the remains of the Zindankale fortress and towers of the city walls, all long since vanished. The sleek vertical line introduced by the elegant minaret (destroyed by lightning in 1901) contrasts with the rough horizontals of the low mud-brick walls and houses. A lone figure, almost invisible, strolls in front of the mosque. All around is ruin, desolation, emptiness. Only in a view of the Sırçalı Medrese façade (1242) do figures play a prominent role in the composition, as two young girls stand before the portal *(plate 42)*.

The Sultan Han (1232–36), the impressive Seljuk caravanserai on the road between Konya and Aksaray, offered Haynes a monument of both intricacy and scale, which he could study from a variety of vantage points *(plates 44–47)*. He took several detailed views of the elaborately sculpted external and internal portals, both covered by elegant *muqarnas* (honeycomb) vaults. He also experimented with angles and vantage points, much as he and Stillman had done at the Parthenon. The view of the internal courtyard, taken from the high enclosure wall, accentuates the spaciousness of the complex, which actually spreads over an area of some 4,500 square metres, while displaying both the rich detail and the state of ruination – the latter emphasised by the view over the walls into the austere plains beyond *(plate 47)*. The careful framing of the photograph actually cuts out the mean squatters' houses within the courtyard – which is to say, the complex was not completely abandoned. The angle of view aligns the band of geometric ornament on the ruined *mescid* (small mosque) at the centre of the photograph with the better-preserved ornamental band framing the entrance to the vaulted hall on its left. It is a stunning picture, marred only by an overexposed band on the right side – a problem Haynes experienced with several photographs.

Inside the cathedral-like hall of the Sultan Han, Haynes used the regular repetition of structural supports and broken vaults to full advantage, emphasising the perspective recession *(plates 44 and 45)*. A companion, probably Sterrett, stands at the back, isolated in a patch of sunlight. Haynes took another, more dramatic photograph from the roof, looking in through the broken vault, from the opposite end of the hall. Again a travelling companion appears in the distance, dwarfed by the immense nave. Contrasts of light and shadow add to the picturesque quality of both interior views, while the repetition of simple architectural volumes contrasts with evidence of decay and weathering. Oddly, for the 1892 album Haynes chose neither of these fine interior views, opting instead for an uninhabited and less dramatic photograph.

At Kayseri, Haynes was fascinated by the simple geometric forms of the Seljuk mausolea outside the city. He took several views of the cylindrical fourteenth-century Sırçalı Kümbet. In one, the building is seen close at hand, again with a colleague, perhaps Sterrett, standing to one side *(plate 69)*. The symmetrical view frames the portals so that we see through it and out of the opposite doorway into the landscape beyond. In a second view, taken from a short distance away, Haynes maintained the symmetrical framing of the monument, as well as the view through aligned portals, but this time he contrasted the monumentality of the mausoleum with the frail tombstones of the adjacent cemetery *(plate 68)*. Artfully framed, the dark, massive cylinder of the *kümbet* (mausoleum) fills the left half of the composition, while the right half opens to limitless space with the merest suggestion of hills behind the cemetery. The composition appears almost completely abstract and uninhabited, except for the stray horses in the cemetery. Both photographs demonstrate Haynes's growing skill with the camera. The view Haynes chose for the 1892 album, however, is something of a compromise *(plate 70)*. The mausoleum is seen from an angle so that two portals are visible and the square base is easily distinguished. From this angle, the tombstones of the cemetery appear in the foreground, and while still irregular, they appear more substantial, and the contrast with the mausoleum is less dramatic. In addition, the landscape setting contributes to the composition, with the round top of the distant hill repeating the hemispherical form of the mausoleum's vault. Although less artful, the selected photograph provides more visual information.

On both of his journeys across Anatolia, Cappadocia was clearly Haynes's favourite subject, and his photographs are the oldest of the region. The evocative combination of the abstract forms of the eroded volcanic landscape and the imagined history of the region fascinated him. We are led into the genuinely picturesque (in the Ruskinian sense) landscape by his team on horseback, who pause while riding across a field north of Göreme *(plate 49)*. An irregular line of eroded cones is silhouetted against the sky behind them. The vantage point is raised, and jagged lines lead our eye into the landscape, composed of dramatic contrasts of light and shadow. In the foreground, where the riders wait, the fields are broad and open, while in the distance the rock forms become increasingly complex. As we follow Haynes's camera into the areas of erosion, we occasionally lose our grounding in reality *(plates 50 and 51)*. The landscape appears vast, hallucinatory and uninhabited; our only reference to human presence or scale is provided by carved doorways or steps cut into the cones. As in some of Turner's late landscapes, reality gives way to abstraction. The combination of monumentality, irregularity and

natural beauty imbues Haynes's Cappadocian photographs with a sense of the sublime. Our imagination is moved to awe, while his subject tends towards formlessness. In the view of dovecotes in the cliffs of the Soğanlı Valley, for example, the patterns are artful and abstract, lacking both human reference and scale *(plate 66)*.

Haynes also revelled in the juxtapositions provided by the careful architectural carving and the unpredictability of nature. In a view of the so-called Tomb of Hieron in Avcılar (Göreme) we see the arched doorway and neatly squared façade cut into the irregular cone *(plate 64)*. The crispness of carving contrasts with the curvilinear eroded forms. The evidence of historic human habitation appears inconsequential within the millennial drama of the Cappadocian landscape.

In one of the few photographs of the Göreme monastic settlement, stairs lead up through a fissure in the rock to an all-but-hidden façade, decorated with horseshoe-shaped arches painted with crosses *(plate 65)*. In his views of the contemporary settlements at Avcılar, Uçhisar, Çavuşin or Ürgüp, Haynes captures the distinctions between the contemporary architectural forms and the weird topography, and between the results of human activity and natural erosion *(plates 56–62)*. The lack of a human presence in many of the Cappadocian photographs accentuates the other-worldly quality of the landscape. Only in his street scenes of Ürgüp do figures play a role. There, however, they are set against the modern town and not the landscape.

For many of his photographs of the highlands of Phrygia, in which he was also recording rock-cut architecture, Haynes similarly depicts the austerity of the landscape, with its curious rock-cut features. Occasionally he took a slightly different approach, situating figures prominently within the landscape. In a view of a Hellenistic tomb, for example, he explores the contrasts of dark and light in the monumental temple-like façade, while positioning one of his travelling companions in the portico, standing heroically in profile *(plate 94)*. The dignity of his pose adds to the dignity of the monument, like that of the solitary horseman on the bridge at Assos. At another monument, travellers pause at the door of the tomb, introducing an element of modernity into the view.

At Assos, Haynes had realised how figures could be introduced into his photographs to dramatic effect. The figures could add a second focal point to the composition, or they could introduce a narrative component. Mimetic actions could add to their visual interest. At the northern Mesopotamian site of Arslan Tash (Lion Stone), a helmeted colleague, possibly the Rev. Dr William Hayes Ward, leader of the Wolfe Expedition, poses with a monumental lion as natives stand about – resembling a wild-game hunter and his conquered prey *(plate 76)*. At the remnants of another site with the same name, the Hittite Aslantaş, Haynes shot one photograph of the lion statues – all that remains – with a companion at one of the lions' heads, then another posing on horseback to simulate the lions' stance *(front cover and plate 78)*.

Rather than introduce human figures at Zincirli, he simply leant his rifle against the stone orthostat blocks for scale *(plate 79)*. At the same time, his modern weapon reflects the ancient one wielded by the warrior represented on the stone immediately behind his gun. A blurry photograph survives of the same subject, but with a gun-wielding *zaptiye* (gendarme) in the place of the gun. Apparently the *zaptiye* did not understand the necessity of holding the pose, thus ruining the photograph. In fact, the picture is much more successful without him. The mimicry is both subtle and effective.

A variety of photographs may be identified as coming from the Wolfe Expedition. They probably include those just noted – all from sites visited by the Americans, although Haynes passed through this region on several occasions. Ward described Arslan Tash in detail, and it is tempting to identify the helmeted gentleman in the photograph as him. Views of Baghdad, Borsippa, Dura, Palmyra and Damascus also seem to come from this trip.

The views of Palmyra are perhaps the most spectacular, although hardly unique, as many others had photographed the picturesque desert city. In many views, Haynes once again shoots from a high vantage point and stresses the grandeur and spaciousness of the ancient city, showing the striking monuments and colonnades from the Roman period along the *decumanus (plate 85)*. In others, he isolates the tomb towers, sometimes framing them to appear aligned in the foreground, middle ground and distance *(plate 115)*. In a more casual view, Haynes's travelling companion the epigrapher Sterrett, apparently recovered from illness, poses amid the ruins *(plate 26)*.

From 1889 onwards, Nippur was the focus of Haynes's photography. Compared with the grand stone monuments of Anatolia and Syria or the strange, carved landscapes of Cappadocia and Phrygia, the mounds and mudflats of southern Mesopotamia are considerably less photogenic. A photograph from the first season showing the Americans' fortified living quarters emphasises the barrenness and desolation of the site *(plate 103)*. Nevertheless, Haynes is able to find a subtle and austere beauty in the setting, and the Babylon Exploration Fund had provided him with improved camera equipment.

By the third season (1893–96), the excavations had progressed to a point where the exposed lower stages of the ziggurat and the continuing excavations in the temple court offer impressive possibilities for Haynes's photography. He presents the site from above, with buildings seen at dramatic angles *(plates 105–107)*. Sometimes he will pull away from the subject, so that the trains of workers appear like ants, dwarfed by the immensity of the architecture and its landscape setting. At other times, he will isolate a sole human being within the landscape *(plate 110)*. Occasionally he toys with the sort of mimesis he used in the Wolfe Expedition photographs. For example, in a posed view of a worker exposing a drainpipe, the angle of the worker's body mirrors that of the ceramic drain *(plate 108)*. In another, the pose of a seated boy reflects the irregular triangle of the arch immediately next to him *(plate 109)*. In others we get a sense of the activities at the site involving both the American team and the locals, such as a festival in which the locals carry Mrs Haynes in a sedan chair *(plate 112)*.

In his last season at Nippur (1898–1900), Haynes's photography became increasingly anthropological, as he attempted to capture aspects of the lives of the local tribes. While these are fascinating images from an anthropological perspective, the Ruskinian picturesque that so informed his earlier works is much less in evidence *(plates 113–114)*. Of all Haynes's work, the anthropological photography has drawn the most interest in recent scholarship, as it recorded a way of life that existed in the marshes until fairly recent times. By 1900, Haynes was at the height of his abilities – both technically and artistically – as a photographer. Then his career abruptly ended.

115 *The Tower Tomb of Elahbel and his three brothers, largest of the tower tombs of Palmyra, was built in AD103. The arch above the door contains a representation of a sarcophagus. Haynes composed this 1885 photograph to include other tower tombs in the middle and far distance*

CODA

When he left archaeology behind in 1900, Haynes also left behind photography, as well as his camera equipment, which in fact belonged to the Babylon Exploration Fund. An accomplished and prolific photographer, Haynes has remained curiously unknown. He often had financial support from the Archaeological Institute of America, and there is a long correspondence with his sponsor, Charles Eliot Norton, the president of the AIA, on the subject. While he provided numerous photographs and negatives to the institute, the AIA no longer maintains a photographic archive. The negatives and photographs from the Wolfe Expedition went to the Metropolitan Museum of Art but were later transferred to the collection of the AIA and have since disappeared from sight.

Haynes did not sign his negatives, as professional photographers often did; nor did he give any indication of authorship on the plates of his 1892 folio. A few university photographic collections have plates from Haynes's folio, but without the booklet to credit them to Haynes. The collections at the University of Pennsylvania and Harvard were both acquired long after Haynes's death. Columbia University has images from the 1892 folio, preserved with the archival materials of William R. Ware, founder of the School of Architecture at Columbia, but these are mixed in with a variety of other images and are unattributed. More are in the archives of the National Geographic Society in Washington, D.C., including some unpublished views, but these are credited to Sterrett, or to Albert T. Clay (who wrote about Nippur in *The National Geographic* in 1916). Those at Cornell University are attributed to Sterrett as well. While there was some attempt after Haynes's death to rehabilitate his reputation as an archaeologist, his contributions to the history of photography never figured in the discussion.

The fault may lie partly with Haynes, who saw himself first and foremost as an archaeologist, a profession in which he was always overshadowed by others. At Assos he was part of a team, and his responsibilities beyond photography were never clearly spelled out. At Nippur he was the discoverer, not the interpreter, the field manager, not the archaeologist in charge. More importantly, in spite of his discerning eye and his artistic sensibility, like his colleagues at Assos, Haynes understood his photography to be little more than a tool of the trade. He saw his photographs as facts, not as interpretations. He failed to appreciate what is obvious to the present viewer: his own, distinctive auteur's vision. In contrast, his teacher, Stillman, was thoroughly grounded in the artistic theories of the day; he published his photography for its artistic merits ('picturesquely and architecturally'), and it was recognised in those terms.

Haynes's work is often similar in character, but even in his 1892 folio, he presents his photographs for their scientific, documentary value, not as works of art. Comparing the photographs he selected to appear in his published album with others he took at the same time, it is clear that he based his selection on the 'information' content of the photographs, rather than their artistic merit, and that he preferred the more 'scientific' images, often without human figures or the suggestion of narrative. In sum, his anonymity as a photographer may be the direct result of the anonymity he ascribed to the photographic process.

Attitudes to photography have changed over the course of the past century. We now view photography as a complex process, for the lens of the camera looks both ways, telling us as much about the person behind it as it does about the subject in front of it. On first discovering the Haynes Collection in the University of Pennsylvania Museum Archives, I was immediately attracted to the views of historical sites and monuments, particularly those significantly altered or destroyed since the late nineteenth century. For the architectural historian, these are of utmost importance, and my concern as a historian was for objective truth and the documentary record. I gradually came to understand the complexity of the choices made by the photographer; for the images came about through his active agency – they are what he chose to represent and how he chose to represent them. They are never neutral, never completely objective. They reflect something of Haynes's values and cultural experience, embedded in a particular moment in time. In turn I, as a viewer, found myself prejudiced by my own cultural values, which influenced the ways I engaged with and ultimately decoded the images.

Doubtless the previous paragraphs would sound very strange to Mr Haynes, the jargon of visual studies all but meaningless. Haynes never attempted to 'theorise' the photographic process. Nevertheless, while he undertook photography as an objective record of the sites and monuments he excavated and visited, his more subjective vision and aesthetic sensibilities shine through and ultimately exalt his photographs. His rapid acquisition of Ruskinian aesthetics from his teacher Stillman seems all the more remarkable, as he extends their application to subject matter probably unimagined by either Stillman or Ruskin. Moreover, the principles Stillman had directed towards the photographic recording of a universally recognised great architectural monument, Haynes took on the road and into the trenches. Through his lens, and through his unique perspective, the archaeological site came to be 'illustrated picturesquely'.

From his writings, Haynes remains something of a cipher, at best a wordy dullard. His photography tells a much richer human story, revealing both a sensitive personality and an artistic vision. Haynes wished to be remembered as the archaeologist who discovered the Temple Library at Nippur, but his contributions to the history of photography are just as substantial and long overdue for recognition.

116 *North Adams, Massachusetts. John Henry Haynes's gravestone, erected in 1913, identifies him simply as 'Archaeological Explorer', while recording an incorrect birth date*

THE AUTHOR

Long involved in the analysis and documentation of the vanishing cultural heritage of the eastern Mediterranean, Robert G. Ousterhout is Professor of Byzantine Art and Architecture at the University of Pennsylvania, where he also directs the Center for Ancient Studies.
He has published more than fifteen books, including *The Art of the Kariye Camii* (Scala, 2002), *A Byzantine Settlement in Cappadocia* (Dumbarton Oaks Studies, 2005; second paperback ed., 2011), *The Byzantine Monuments of the Evros/Meriç River Valley* (Thessaloniki, 2007, with Ch. Bakirtzis) and *Master Builders of Byzantium* (second paperback edition, University of Pennsylvania Museum Publications, 2008), and he is a regular contributor to *Cornucopia Magazine*.

ACKNOWLEDGEMENTS

I am particularly grateful to archivist Alessandro Pezzati at the University of Pennsylvania Museum of Archaeology and Anthropology, who first introduced me to Mr Haynes and helped me in many ways throughout this project. András Riedlmayer, Jeff Spurr and Joanne Bloom assisted me with Haynes's photographs from the Aga Khan Program Documentation Center at Harvard. Bill Bonner and Mimi Dornack did the same at the National Geographic Society. My thanks to them and to the organisations they represent for permissions to reproduce the images in this book. The Stillman photographs come courtesy of the Gennadius Library at the American School of Classical Studies at Athens, and I thank Dr Maria Georgopoulou for assistance in locating them and Prof. Andrew Szegedy-Maszak for sharing his knowledge of them. Kevin Mullen and Brian Johnson assisted with Haynes's letters at the AIA and American Board archives respectively; Linda Hall located Haynes's class photo from Williams College. A Halpern-Rogath Curatorial Seminar at the University of Pennsylvania provided ample opportunity to develop and refine my ideas about Haynes – and to teach myself about the history of photography – while preparing the exhibition *Archaeologists and Travelers in Ottoman Lands* for the University of Pennsylvania Museum and its second iteration at the Pera Museum in Istanbul as *Osman Hamdi Bey and the Americans*. I am indebted in very many ways to Özalp Birol and the Suna and İnan Kıraç Foundation for their assistance with this project. My co-curator and co-conspirator Renata Holod has provided a wealth of good ideas and sound advice. Our seminar students offered many insightful observations, and I owe special thanks to Elvan Cobb, Victoria Fleck, Theodore Van Loan and Jamie Sanecki. Finally, I am obliged to my good friends Nina Joukowsky Köprülü, John Scott, Berrin Torolsan and Brian Rose for their continued support and encouragement. For the second edition, I add my gratitude to Benjamin Anderson and the staff of the Kroch Library for making the materials at Cornell University available, and to Kathy Seligman and the Rowe Historical Society for information on the early life of Haynes.

BIBLIOGRAPHY

Allen, Susan Heuck, *Excavating Our Past: Perspectives on the History of the Archaeological Institute of America* (Boston, 2002)

Clarke, Joseph Thacher, *Preliminary Report of the Investigations at Assos During the Year 1881* (Boston, 1882)

—— *Report on the Investigations at Assos, 1882, 1883* (New York, 1898).

Clarke, Joseph Thacher, Francis Bacon and Robert Koldewey *Investigations at Assos* (Cambridge, MA, 1902–21)

Frith, Susan, 'The Rise and Fall of Hermann Hilprecht', *The Pennsylvania Gazette* (Jan.–Feb. 2003)

Geere, H. Valentine, *By Nile and Euphrates: A Record of Discovery and Adventure* (London, 1904)

Hilprecht, Herman V., *Explorations in Bible Lands during the 19th Century* (Philadelphia, 1903)

—— *The So-called Peters–Hilprecht Controversy* (Philadelphia, 1908).

Holod, Renata, and Robert Ousterhout, eds., *Archaeologists and Travelers in Ottoman Lands*, online exhibition catalogue (Philadelphia, 2010)

Kuklick, Bruce. *Puritans in Babylon: The Ancient Near East and American Intellectual Life, 1800–1930* (Princeton, 1996)

Lawton, William C., 'From Venice to Assos', *The Atlantic Monthly* 63 (April 1889), 500–09

Lyons, Claire L., John K. Papadopoulos, Lindsey S. Stewart, and Andrew Szegedy-Mascak, *Antiquity & Photography: Early Views of Ancient Mediterranean Sites* (Los Angeles, 2006)

Ochsenschlager, Edward L., *Iraq's Marsh Arabs in the Garden of Eden* (Philadelphia, 2004), esp. 251–69 for Haynes's anthropological photography

Ousterhout, Robert, *Palmyra 1885* (Edinburgh, 2016)

—— 'Archaeologists and Travelers in Ottoman Lands: Three Intersecting Lives', *Expedition* 52/2 (2010), 9–20

—— 'On the Road to Ruins', *Cornucopia* 44 (2010), 38–57.

Peters, John P., *Nippur or Explorations and Adventures on the Euphrates*, 2 vols (New York, 1897, 1904)

Sterrett, John Robert Sitlington, *Preliminary Report on an Epigraphical Journey Made in Asia Minor during the Summer of 1884* (Boston, 1885).

—— 'Troglodyte Dwellings in Cappadocia', *The Century* 60 (1900), 677–87

—— 'The Cone Dwellers of Asia Minor: A Primitive People Who Live in Nature-Made Apartment Houses Fashioned by Volcanic Violence and Trickling Streams', *The National Geographic Magazine* 35/4 (1919), 281–331

Stillman, William James, *The Autobiography of a Journalist*, 2 vols. (Boston, 1901)

Ward, William Hayes, *Report on the Wolfe Expedition to Babylonia 1884–85* (Boston, 1886)

Zettler, Richard L., 'Excavations at Nippur, the University of Pennsylvania, and the University Museum' in *Nippur at the Centennial*, ed. Maria deJong Ellis (Philadelphia, 1992), 325–36

SOURCES

While the AIA no longer has a photographic archive, they preserve the substantial correspondence from Haynes to Norton at their Boston office. Surviving photographs from Haynes's personal collection are divided between the archives of the University of Pennsylvania Museum of Archaeology and Anthropology and the Documentation Center of the Aga Khan Program for Islamic Architecture at the Fine Arts Library, Harvard University – the latter purchased on eBay from his descendants. His travel diaries and letters are similarly divided. Official correspondence from Aintab is preserved in the archives of the American Board of Christian Foreign Missions in Istanbul, recently transferred to the library of the American Research Institute in Turkey, Istanbul Branch. Photographs, glass plate negatives, field reports and substantial correspondence from Nippur are housed in the University of Pennsylvania Museum Archives. Another 300 photographs, primarily from the Wolfe Expedition are house in Special Collections at the Cornell University Library, all attributed to Sterrett. Doubtless there is more waiting to be discovered.

PICTURE CREDITS

CORNELL UNIVERSITY LIBRARY
Division of Rare and Manuscript Collections
48, 77, 81, 82, 83, 85
HAK ARCHIVES
Harvard University, Documentation Center of the Aga Khan
Program for Islamic Architecture, courtesy of Special Collections,
Fine Arts Library
25, 27, 28, 33, 34, 46, 47 (frontispiece), 51, 54, 55, 58, 59, 61, 62,
65, 66, 70, 72, 73, 86, 87, 88, 89, 90, 91, 92, 93, 94, 95, 96, 97, 98.
NGS ARCHIVES
National Geographic Society, Washington, D.C.,
photographic archives
52, 53.
THE ROWE HISTORICAL SOCIETY
1D.
UPM ARCHIVES
University of Pennsylvania Museum of Archaeology and
Anthropology, Philadelphia, PA, Archives
1A, 1C, 5, 6, 7, 8, 9, 10, 11, 12, 13, 14, 15, 16, 17, 18, 19, 20, 21,
22, 23, 24, 26, 29, 30, 31, 32, 35, 36, 37, 38, 39, 40, 41, 42, 43, 44,
45, 49, 56, 57, 60, 63, 64, 67, 68, 69, 71, 74, 75, 78, 79, 80, 84,
99, 100, 101, 102, 103, 104, 105, 106, 107, 108, 109, 110, 111,
112, 113, 114, 115 all inside cover images.
WILLIAMS COLLEGE ARCHIVES AND SPECIAL COLLECTIONS,
WILLIAMSTOWN, MA
Back cover.
WIKIPEDIA COMMONS
1B.
GENNADIUS LIBRARY, AMERICAN SCHOOL OF CLASSICAL STUDIES,
ATHENS, GREECE
2, 3, 4.
JAMIE SANECKI
116.

TEXT © Robert G. Ousterhout 2016

Robert G. Ousterhout has asserted his right
to be identified as the author of this work.

A CORNUCOPIA BOOK
FIRST PUBLISHED 2011 by Caique Publishing Ltd
1 Rutland Court, Edinburgh EH3 8EY
in association with Kayık Yayıncılık Ltd
Valikonağı Caddesi 64, Nişantaşı, 34367 Istanbul
2ND EDITION 2016

ISBN 978-0-9565948-6-0

PROJECT EDITORS John Scott, Berrin Torolsan
TEXT EDITORS Susana Raby, Rose Shepherd, Tony Barrell,
Hilary Stafford-Clark
DESIGN Clive Crook and Debi Angel
SPECIAL IMAGING Orhan Gündüz

PRINTED AND BOUND IN TURKEY
by Ofset Yapımevi, Istanbul
www.ofset.com

CORNUCOPIA BOOKS
PO Box 13311, Hawick TD9 7YF
www.cornucopia.net